- HERGÉ -
★

THE ADVENTURES OF TINTIN

THE SHOOTING STAR

EGMONT

Original Album: *The Shooting Star*

Translated by Leslie Lonsdale-Cooper and Michael Turner

Additional Material

www.casterman.com
www.tintin.com

This edition published in 2013 by Egmont UK Ltd.
The Yellow Building,
1 Nicholas Road, London W11 4AN

egmont.co.uk

1 3 5 7 9 10 8 6 4 2
ISBN: 978 1 4052 6701 4

55036/1

Tintin

A bright new star, shining in the night sky, marks the beginning of a brand new adventure for brave reporter Tintin.

Snowy

No matter how bad things get, Tintin's faithful dog, Snowy, is scared of nothing...except spiders!

Philippulus the Prophet

Philippulus the Prophet loves banging his drum and forecasting doom and gloom. It almost seems like he's looking forward to the end of the world!

Professor Decimus Phostle

There's nothing Professor Phostle hates more than a mistaken calculation... even when it means that it is not the end of the world!

Captain Haddock

Tintin and Professor Phostle need a ship to hunt for the meteorite that has fallen into the sea. But who will be in command of the vessel? Enter Tintin's new friend, Captain Haddock!

Mr Bohlwinkel

Mr Bohlwinkel is intent on exploiting the meteorite for his own financial gain.
Bohlwinkel uses his international business network
in attempts to thwart Tintin's team!

Captain Chester

Just when it looks like Tintin and Captain Haddock have been beaten, one of Haddock's old friends, Captain Chester, shows up to help!

THE SHOOTING STAR

Hello? Is that the observatory? Can you tell me . . . I've just noticed a very large, bright star in the Great Bear . . . I wonder . . .

Hello? . . . What? . . . You have the phenomenon under observation? I see . . . And . . . Hello? . . . Hello? . . . Hello? . . . They've hung up!

Very odd! Why did they ring off so abruptly? . . . Crumbs, how hot it is! Phew! . . .

?

I can't believe my eyes! It's getting bigger every minute!

All very peculiar . . . and I'm going to get to the bottom of it. Come on, Snowy . . . to the Observatory.

RRRRING
OBSERVATORY

Definitely, it's bigger than ever! . . .

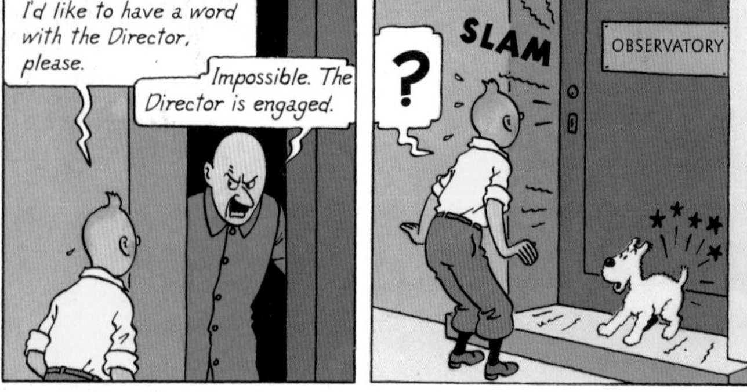
I'd like to have a word with the Director, please.
Impossible. The Director is engaged.

SLAM
OBSERVATORY
?

That's the limit! Slamming the door in my face!
What a nerve!
RRRRING
RRING

You again? . . . I told you before, the Director's engaged. He can't . . .
That doesn't matter now . . . The Observatory's on fire! . . .

Good gracious! Where?
Here, come and look . . .

?!
SLAM

How strangely quiet and empty it all is . . . as if there weren't a soul . . .

Ah, there's somebody.
A judgement! Woe!

Excuse me, sir, could you tell me . . .
That's what I told them: "It's a judgement."

A judgement! Yea! . . . A judgement, and don't you forget it!
?
?

NO ENTRY

NO ENTRY
RAT
RAT
TAT

RAT
TAT
NO ENTR
TAT
TAT
TAT

Excuse me, I'm looking for the Director of the Observatory.
Ssh! It's me!

It's me, but ssh! . . . Silence! Don't disturb my colleague; he's deep in some very complicated mathematics. While he's finishing, have a look through the telescope, if you like; it's a sight worth seeing.

Let's have a look.

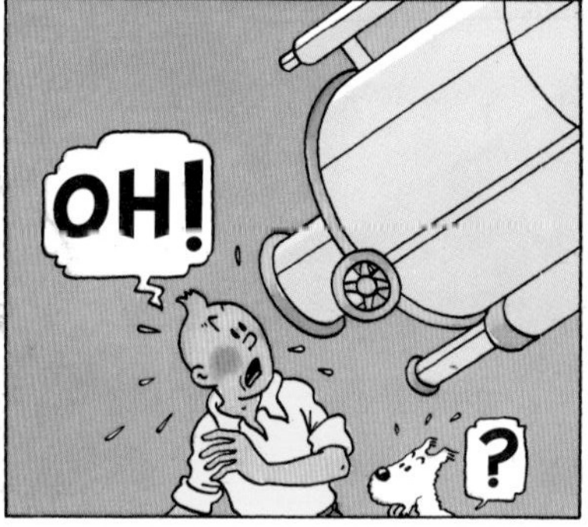
OH!
?

Good heavens, sir! It's horrible . . . horrible!
Yes, in one sense it's horrible . . .

It's enormous! Simply enormous!
Enormous, yes!

And its hairy legs! . . . It makes me shiver to think of them!
Its legs? . . . What legs?

What legs? . . . Why, belonging to that gigantic spider . . .
Spider? . . . Is this your idea of a joke young man?

Come and see for yourself!

By the rings of Saturn! . . . You're right . . . It is, quite definitely, a spider! . . .
You see now!

How extraordinary! Extraordinary! . . . It has characteristics of Meta segmentata . . . At least . . . No! It's an Araneus diadematus! An enormous Araneus diadematus!

Anyway, it's a spider! Ugh! What a monster! . . . And it's travelling through space . . . Supposing it . . . ??

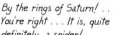

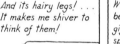

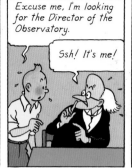

Hello, Professor . . . I've found the answer . . . It was a spider walking across the lens! . . . It's gone now . . .

A spider? . . . A harmless little spider! That's all it was, scaring them out of their wits! . . . This'll kill me!

WOOAH!

Come and look now . . .

Well?

It looks like . . . It looks like a huge ball of fire . . .

It IS a ball of fire! . . . A VA-A-A-A-AST ball of fire . . .
?

Yes, it's a gigantic mass of matter in fusion . . .
But why is it growing bigger . . . before our very eyes? . . . Because it is growing, isn't it?

Naturally it's growing bigger – it's heading towards us, at an incredible speed.
Heading towards us? . . . But if it keeps on coming . . . ?

Yes! . . . That fire-ball is going to collide with the Earth!
Great heavens! But that'll mean . . .

. . . THE END OF THE WORLD, YES!

I've finished, sir. Here are the calculations. The collision will take place tomorrow morning at 08.12 hours and 30 seconds precisely.

The end of the world . . .
. . . At 8.12 ½ a.m. . . . That's good . . . and I, Decimus Phostle, have determined the moment at which the cataclysm will befall us! Tomorrow I shall be famous!

But . . . It's impossible . . . You . . . I mean . . . Perhaps you made a mistake in your calculations.
Sir!!!
Made a mistake? Us? You presume to . . . ? Very well! Check them!

!

I . . . I'm sure they're all correct Professor! . . . I'll take your word for it! Goodbye!

The end of the world!

Hey, Snowy? What's the matter?
HELP!

Just in time!

Rats! . . . Millions of rats coming up from the sewers! . . . Absolutely panic-stricken!

Whew! . . . They've gone! . . . What about Snowy? What's happened to him?

Snowy!

BANG
BANG
?

The tyres . . . they've burst, from the terrific heat . . .

SNOWY! . . . SNOWY!

Oh, so there you are! Well? What are you doing there? Why don't you come when I call you? Come here!

Great snakes! He . . . he can't move . . . It looks . . . It looks as if he's paralysed!
Help, Tintin, Help!

My poor Snowy!

What on earth . . . ? Oh, now I see! This frightful heat has melted the tar . . .

Confound the star!

Poor things! . . . If only they knew! . . .

DONG
DONG
DONG
DONG
DONG
?

Judgement is upon us! Repent! The end of the world is at hand!
?

I am Philippulus the prophet! I proclaim the day of terror! . . . The end of the world is nigh! All men will perish! . . . And the survivors will die of hunger and cold! . . . There will be pestilence, and famine, and measles!

Look here Mr Prophet, why don't you go home? You'd be better off in bed! . . .
!

You hear that? He dares to set himself up against Philippulus the prophet . . . An advocate of the devil! . . . A son of Satan! . . . A tool of Beelzebub!

Get back to Satan, your Master!

Oyez, there will be a plague! Bubonic plague! . . . and fever! The end of the world is upon us, servant of Satan!
That fellow gets on my nerves!

Here we are, home at last!

What a blinding light!

OWW!
?

Crumbs! The window frame is so hot I burnt myself! . . .

Poor old Snowy . . . dying for a drink. And that poor little plant's all wilted.

The end of the world, Snowy! . . . The END of the world! . . . The end of the WORLD! D'you understand, Snowy?

DONG
DONG

Return to your Master, the Prince of Darkness!

There! . . . Now I hope he'll leave me in peace!

I think I'll have a bit of a rest. I'm absolutely worn out . . .

Phew! . . . I've had enough of this.

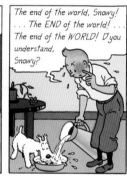

. . . seconds . . . pip . . . pip . . . pip . . . At the third stroke it will be eight twelve and twenty seconds . . . Pip . . . pip . . . pip . . . At the third stroke it will be eight twelve and thirty seconds . . . pip . . . pip . . .

Help!

We're dead! . . .

No! . . . On second thoughts, we aren't dead . . . and it isn't the end of the world . . . It's nothing but an earthquake!
Oh? . . . Is THAT all it is?

I wonder how they'll explain this one at the Observatory! . . . Hello? . . . Hello? . . . Hello? . . . The telephone's not working. . . . Come on Snowy, we're going along there.

Hooray! . . . Hooray! It's only an earthquake! . . .

RRRING RRRRRRING RRING
OBSERVATOR

RRRING RRRRRING RRING RRING RRRRRING
All right! All right! I'm coming!

Hooray! Hooray! . . . The end of the world has been postponed!

Hooray! Hooray! . . . It's good to be alive!

NO ENTRY
RAT TAT

NO ENTRY

Bungler! . . . Dunderhead!
What has he done?

The idiot! He made a mistake in his calculations! The meteor passed 48,000 km away from the earth, instead of colliding with it and causing the magnificent cataclysm I'd hoped for.
Never mind, Professor; you've still got it in store . . . But tell me: what about the earthquake?

Professor! . . . Professor! . . .

It has just been developed, sir. It is indeed remarkable, don't you agree, sir?
Excellent! . . . Excellent! . . . But, look there. How very extraordinary!

That group of lines, in the centre? Uranium, I presume.
Uranium? Not on your life! . . .
?

By the rings of Saturn! It's prodigious!

Tralala ♪ ♪ - la ♪
It may be prodigious, but it's all Greek to me!

It's prodigious! . . . Incredible! . . . Fantastic! . . . Stupefying!

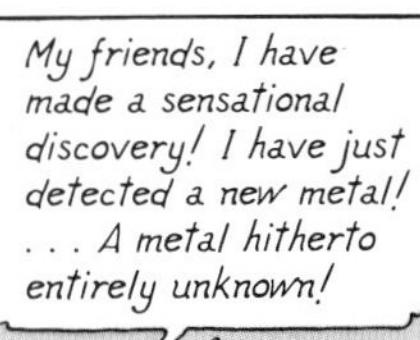
My friends, I have made a sensational discovery! I have just detected a new metal! . . . A metal hitherto entirely unknown!

You've heard of the spectroscope. It's the instrument that enables us to discover elements in stars, elements not yet isolated here on the earth. This is a spectroscopic photograph of the meteor which brushed past us today. Each of these lines, or each group of lines is characteristic of a metal. Those lines in the centre represent an unknown metal, which exists in the meteor. You follow me?
Er . . . more or less . . .

I, Decimus Phostle, have discovered a new metal! I shall give my name to it: phostlite.
My heartiest congratulations!

But Professor, to get back to the meteor . . . It didn't collide with the earth, so why was there an earthquake?

Tell me, young man, do you like bull's-eyes?
?

Answer me. Do you or do you not like bull's-eyes?
I . . . er . . . Bull's-eyes? . . . I . . . Yes, thank you . . . but . . .

Go out and buy ten penny-worth of bull's eyes! We must have a fitting celebration of my discovery!

You were asking about the earthquake? . . . Oh, yes . . . It was caused by part of the meteor crashing to earth. As soon as we know where it fell, there we shall find phostlite!

Professor! . . . Professor! Listen to this . . .

"The polar station on Cape Morris (on the northern coast of Greenland) reports that a meteorite has undoubtedly fallen in the Arctic Ocean. Seal-hunters saw a ball of fire cross the sky and disappear over the horizon. A few seconds later the earth shook violently and icebergs cracked . . ."
By the rings of Saturn!

It has fallen into the sea! . . . It has been engulfed by the waves! And with it, my discovery! Proof of the existence of phostlite.
So that's that, Snowy. The phostlite's sunk.

This is the end! My meteorite! My phostlite!
Come on, Snowy, we'll leave him.

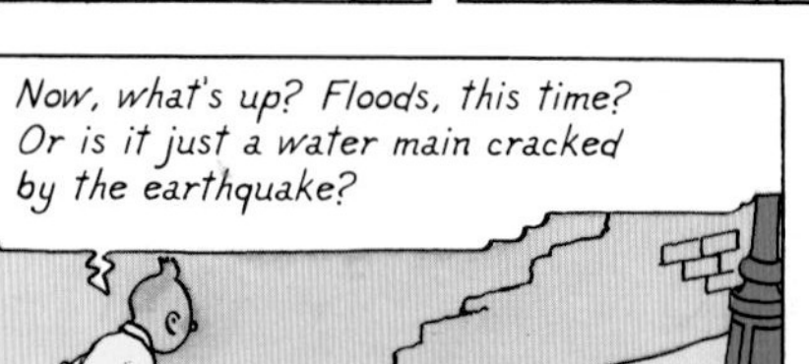

Poor Professor Phostle. He's terribly upset because his meteorite's fallen into the sea.
He's even forgotten to give us a bull's-eye.
OBSERVATORY
Now, what's up? Floods, this time? Or is it just a water main cracked by the earthquake?

These bricks will make stepping stones to keep my feet dry.

SPLASH

Great snakes! Why on earth didn't we think of it before?
?

You see this brick, Snowy?
Of course I can see it! . . .

Watch! . . .

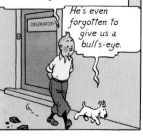

We must make a search and find the meteorite. We must organise an expedition. I'm sure we shall be able to obtain the capital we need from the European Foundation for Scientific Research.

Some time later . . .

A scientific expedition including leading European experts is leaving shortly on a voyage of discovery in Arctic waters. Its objective is to find the meteorite which recently fell in the Arctic region. It is believed that a part of the meteorite may be protruding above the surface of the water and the ice . . .

The expedition will be led by Professor Phostle, who has revealed the presence of an unknown metal in the meteorite. The other members of the party are:

. . . the Swedish scholar Eric Björgenskjöld, author of distinguished papers on solar prominences;

. . . Señor Porfirio Bolero y Calamares, of the University of Salamanca;

. . . Herr Doktor Otto Schulze, of the University of Munich;

. . . Professor Paul Cantonneau, of the University of Paris;

. . . Senhor Pedro Joàs Dos Santos, a renowned physicist, of the University of Coimbra;

. . . Tintin, the young reporter, who will represent the press;

. . . and lastly, Captain Haddock, President of the S.S.S. (Society of Sober Sailors) who will command the "Aurora", the vessel in which the expedition will embark.

Three days later . . .

Well, Snowy, the "Aurora" sails tomorrow.

We'll go aboard for our last night before setting off for Arctic waters.

I don't think much of this expedition; it'll be jolly cold up there.

Hello . . . someone's running down the gangplank . . . That's funny . . . Stop! Who are you?
Hey there! . . . Stop!

Stop! . . .

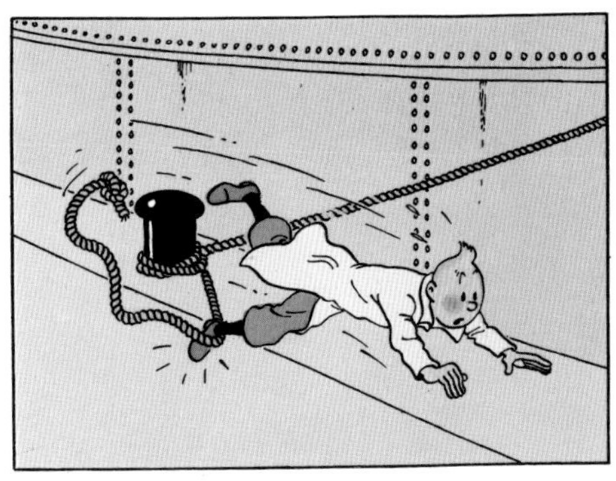

Confound that rope! . . . He's vanished . . . Now, I wonder what that fellow was doing aboard ship.

Are you on watch?
Yes.

You haven't seen anyone prowling around the deck?
No.

Oh! . . . Good! . . . Er . . . Is Captain Haddock in his cabin?
Yes.

Yes . . . No . . . Not very communicative!

Hello, where's Snowy got to? . . . Snowy . . . Snowy! SNOWY!

!

RAT
TAT
TAT
TAT
Come in.

Hello, Captain. I've just seen a man bolting off the ship. He made off when I challenged him! . . .
?

Wooah! . . . Wooah! . . . Wooah! . . .

Ah, there you are Snowy! Hey, what are you doing?
I'd say he wants us to follow him . . .

Wooah! Wooah!

Dynamite! . . . Lucky for us someone put out the fuse!
Good old Snowy! . . . He . . . well, he did his best, Captain . . .

Someone wanted to blow up the ship, or at least damage it badly. But why? . . .
One thing, if I ever lay hands on that Pyromaniac, he'll see a good display of fireworks!

Anyway, we must be on our guard. I suggest you go the rounds.
A good idea . . .

Yes, we must keep our eyes open.

?

You gangster, you! . . . You won't escape me!

I've got you, you rat!
Help! Help!
DYNAMITER!
SHIPWRECKER!

Come on out, centipede! Let's see you in the daylight!

Good gracious! It's Professor Phostle!
I shall complain! I shall complain to the Captain!

Professor Phostle, allow me to introduce Captain Haddock . . . You must excuse him, but we've just discovered an attempt at sabotage . . .
An attempt at sabotage? Can that be possible?
Yes, a stick of dynamite on the deck!

Fortunately Snowy had the sense to put out the fuse. But come and see . . .

?
What is it?

The dynamite! It's gone! . . .
?
Thundering typhoons!

It was there only two minutes ago! . . . I simply can't understand it.
Extraordinary!

DING
DING
DING

DING
DING
DING
DING
Hey! The ship's bell!

Did you pick something up from the deck there? . . .
No . . .

Nobody here!

Ahoy there! Captain . . .
!
Someone's calling.

I am Professor Cantonneau. I would like to speak to the Captain.
That's me. I'll come down.

BANG
?

Professor Cantonneau! What has happened to him?
I've no idea. Perhaps he tripped over. His suitcase is smashed to bits . . .
He's alive!

But . . . that's my suitcase! . . . MY suitcase. I left it in your cabin.

Tell us, Professor; what happened?
I . . . I . . . don't know . . . A . . . frightful blow . . . like some huge weight falling on my head . . .

HA!
HA!
HA!
HA!
HA!

Ha! ha! ha! ha!

It is the judgement come upon you! Philippulus the prophet gave you warning!

He did it! . . . He dropped the suitcase!
And here is a pretty rocket I found. Now we'll have a beautiful fireworks display! . . .

The dynamite! The crazy fool! He's taken the dynamite! . . . We'll all blow up!

There's not a moment to lose!

There! . . . In half a minute this will go "whoosh"! . . .

I'm sorry. I take no orders, except from above! I'm staying here!

Come down, by thunder, or I'll have you clapped in irons!
Don't argue any more. I know how to bring him down.

?

You'll see. He'll come down at once . . .

Hello, hello, Philippulus the prophet! This is your guardian angel, speaking from heaven. I order you to return to earth. And be careful: don't break your neck!

Yes, sir. At once, sir. Don't be angry, sir . . .

There he is!

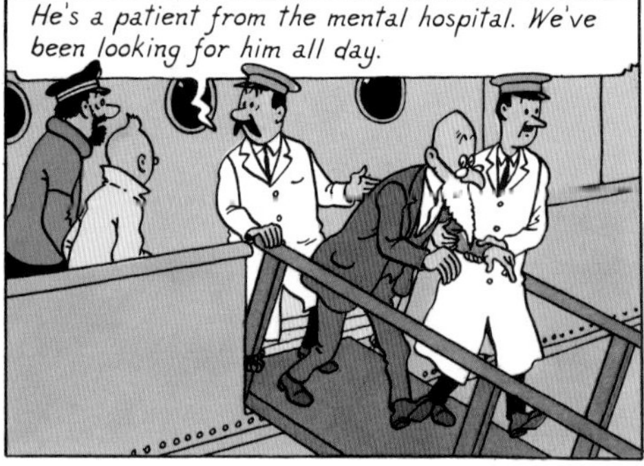
He's a patient from the mental hospital. We've been looking for him all day.

Next morning . . .
There's quite a crowd to see the "Aurora" sail.
WHARF 9

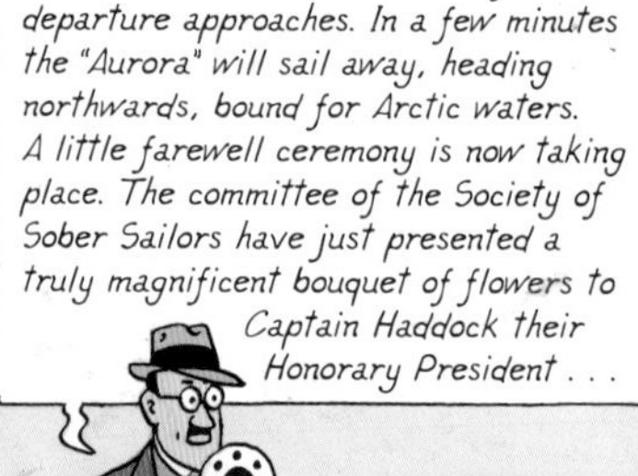
And so, listeners, the moment of departure approaches. In a few minutes the "Aurora" will sail away, heading northwards, bound for Arctic waters. A little farewell ceremony is now taking place. The committee of the Society of Sober Sailors have just presented a truly magnificent bouquet of flowers to Captain Haddock their Honorary President . . .

Goodbye, Captain, most worthy President. Never forget, the eyes of the whole world and the S.S.S. will be upon you. Good luck!

Beg pardon, Captain. Shall we put them in your cabin?
Put what, my lad?

Those . . .
WHISKY
WHISKY
WHISK
WHISK

. . . and here's the President of the European Foundation for Scientific Research with the leader of the expedition, Professor Phostle, handing over the flag to be planted on the meteorite.
E.F.S.R.

. . . I entrust this flag to you, Professor, confident that it will soon fly from the summit of the meteorite. I am sure you will find it, and also the new metal, whose existence you have already announced.

Captain!
Captain! . . .

There's something funny going on . . .

Thundering typhoons!

Read this, Professor. My radio operator has just picked up this signal . . . He intercepted it quite by accident, while he was testing his equipment . . .

São Rico. The polar ship "Peary" sailed from São Rico yesterday evening on a voyage of exploration in Arctic waters. The "Peary" will try to find the meteorite which fell in that area and which, according to experts, contains an unknown metal . . .

They've stolen a march on us! They'll take possession of the meteorite! All is lost . . .
Hold on, they haven't found it yet!

Tintin's right. We've still got a chance . . .

ALL HANDS ABOARD SHIP! . . . We sail at once!

Stand by to cast off!
E.F.S.R.

TOOOOOT

The last moorings have been cast off. This is the moment of departure . . . The ship is moving slowly away from the quay. The "Aurora" has sailed . . . Sailed away in search of a shooting star . . .

You have been listening to an eyewitness account of the departure of the polar research ship "Aurora". The programme was relayed through all European networks.
Ha! ha! ha! I wish them the best of luck!
You're quite sure that they won't succeed? . . .

My dear fellow, you've been my secretary long enough to know that if the Bohlwinkel Bank has financed the "Peary" expedition, there is no question of failure. Believe me: the "Aurora" hasn't a chance.
I hope so, Mr Bohlwinkel. But still . . .

Yes I know the "Aurora" sailed sooner than I anticipated . . . The fault of that fool Hayward, bungling his job. But don't worry, I've taken care of everything . . .
Ah, good good . . .

You see, my dear fellow, the scientific expedition is just a cover for my plan to take possession of this meteorite . . . and the unknown metal Professor Phostle was naive enough to tell us about. There's a colossal fortune waiting there for us. A colossal fortune, and I don't intend to lose it!

We're on our way, Snowy . . .
AURORA

This will blow away the cobwebs, eh, Snowy? What wonderful air . . . the real tang of the sea!
Yes, you can smell the fish . . .

Do as I do, Snowy. Breathe deeply. Fill your lungs with fresh air.

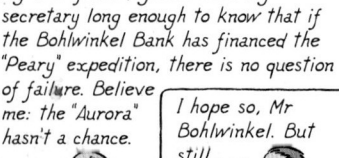

Let's go aft to the stern, Snowy. Anyway, it'll soon be time for lunch . . .

AURORA

Look, Snowy, there's our seaplane up there, on its catapult. It will help in our search for the meteorite.

?

Ahoy there, steward! . . . You can announce lunch. Everything's ready.

First service for luncheon!

Where's Snowy got to? I don't see him about.

Hey, steward, what's the meaning of this? The menu says "Sausages and Mash"! Right: where are the sausages?

They'll find their sea-legs in a day or two . . .

That night . . .

Impossible to sleep a wink . . . She's rolling worse than ever . . . fairly dancing a jig!

Meanwhile, in São Rico . . .
Any further news of the "Kentucky Star"?
Nothing more, Mr Bohlwinkel . . .

I've a good mind to go and join the Captain on the bridge.

Come on, Snowy we'll go to the bridge.

Great snakes! . . . It's blowing a real gale!

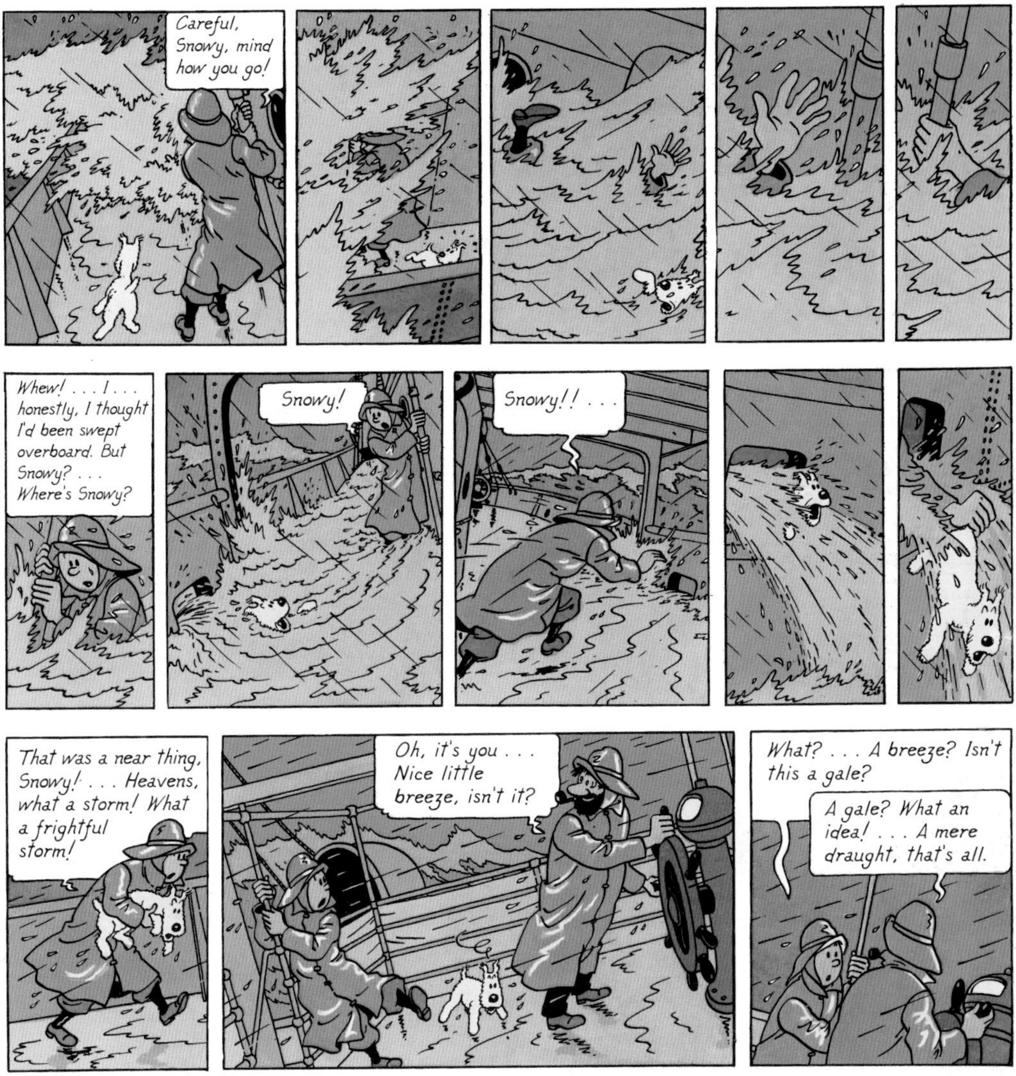

Careful, Snowy, mind how you go!

Whew! . . . I . . . honestly, I thought I'd been swept overboard. But Snowy? . . . Where's Snowy?

Snowy!

Snowy!! . . .

That was a near thing, Snowy! . . . Heavens, what a storm! What a frightful storm!

Oh, it's you . . . Nice little breeze, isn't it?

What? . . . A breeze? Isn't this a gale?

A gale? What an idea! . . . A mere draught, that's all.

Hard a starboard! . . .

AURORA

Pirates! . . . Shipwreckers! . . .
Sea-lice! . . . Filibusters! . . .
Hoodlums! . . . Road-hogs! . . .
Freshwater swabs!
Saved!

The lunatic! A little bit closer and he'd have cut us in two . . . He must be crazy sailing like that, without any lights . . . He couldn't have judged it better if he'd meant to sink us.
And why not? That might be precisely what he intended.

What do you mean?
I mean, Captain, that someone's already tried to sabotage the "Aurora" . . . the night before we sailed. The accident we just avoided looks remarkably like another attempt . . .

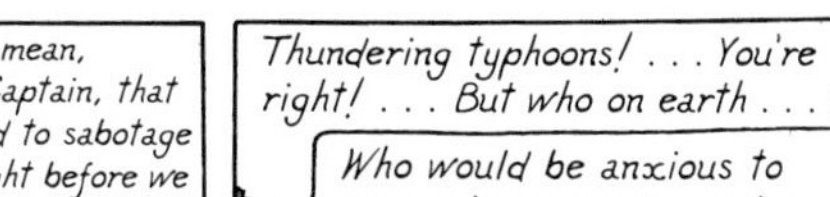

Thundering typhoons! . . . You're right! . . . But who on earth . . . ?
Who would be anxious to prevent us carrying out our search? Who but the "Peary" expedition, or whoever has financed it? . . .

Is that the "Kentucky Star" this time?
Yes, coming in now Mr Bohlwinkel. A radio signal . . .

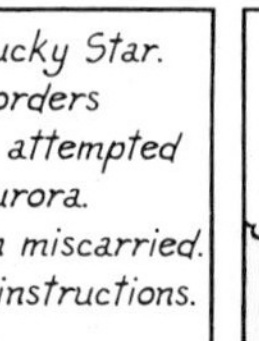
S.S. Kentucky Star. Obeying orders received, attempted to sink Aurora. Operation miscarried. Awaiting instructions.

They've failed! The bungling fools! Now we're back where we started! . . . But I'll get them yet!

Oh, misery! I feel so ill! I feel horribly ill!
I feel sick . . . Ooooooh . . .

Would you mind if I opened the window a little bit? Some fresh air would do us good.
Do as you please . . . just let me die in peace.

Aaaah! . . . I feel better already.

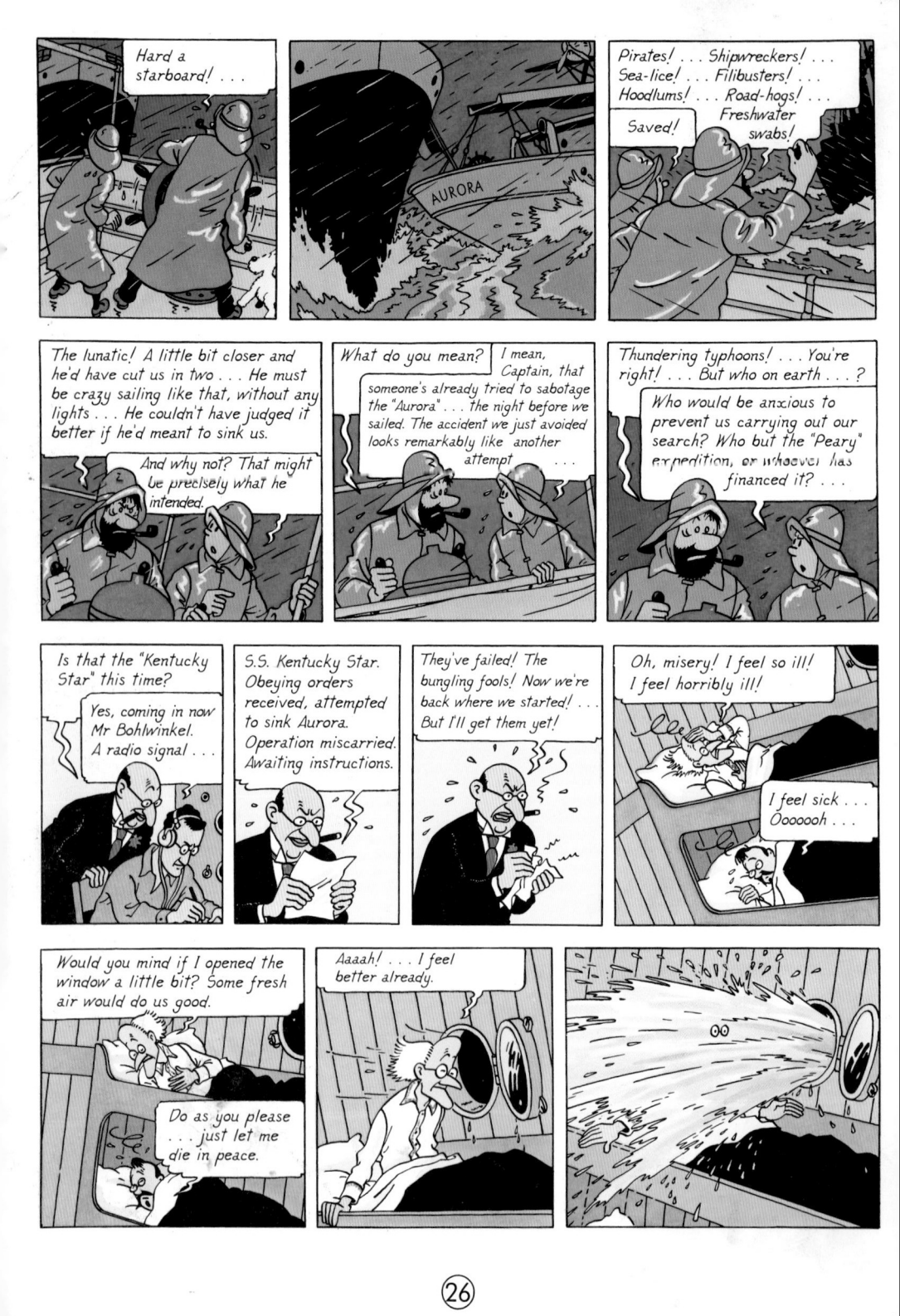

Some days later . . .
Brrr! It's cold this morning. It feels as if we're approaching the Arctic region.

Have you noticed? It froze last night.

You ought to put on warm clothes: you'll catch cold going about like that.
You're quite right.

Come along, Snowy. We need our coats on.

I should have told him to be careful on the deck. This sheet-ice is really . . .

. . . dangerous!

Now we'll go and say good morning to the Captain.
I'm going to cause a sensation!

Here, send this by radio.
Aye, aye, captain.

M.S. Aurora to President, E.F.S.R. In sight of Iceland. Putting into port at Akureyri, in Eyjafjördur, for refuelling. All well on board.

Here, Mr Bohlwinkel: it's a message sent by the "Aurora" to the European Foundation for Scientific Research. Our wireless operator just intercepted it.
Give it me.

Aha! . . . They're putting in at an Icelandic port! Excellent! Excellent! I think, my dear Johnson, that their stay will be a long one . . . Let us begin by sending a short note. Take this down, Johnson . . .
I'm ready, sir . . .

Bohlwinkel Bank to Smithers, general agent for Golden Oil, Reykjavik, Iceland. Circulate following order immediately to all agents for Golden Oil in Iceland: Absolute prohibition against refuelling polar vessel Aurora . . . There! Have that sent in the secret code.
Right, Mr Bohlwinkel.

The next morning . . .
STOP
STAND BY
SLOW
HALF
FULL
AHEAD
ASTERN
FINISHED WITH ENGINES

So here we are in Akureyri. Shall we be staying here long, Captain?
Oh, no . . .

Just long enough to fill up with oil. Then we set out for Greenland.

There. I'm going to order the fuel. It won't take a minute.
GOLDEN OIL
Right. I'll wait for you here.

Good morning. I want my ship refuelled with oil.
Very good. What's the name of your vessel?

Polar research ship "Aurora". Captain Haddock.
Oh? . . . You're the Captain of . . . of the "Aurora"?

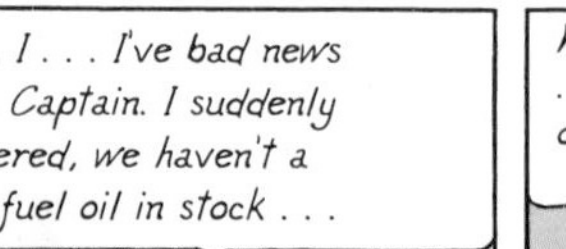

Oh! . . . I . . . I've bad news for you, Captain. I suddenly remembered, we haven't a drop of fuel oil in stock . . .
?

What's that you say? No fuel oil? . . . That's absurd! I've got to have oil, d'you hear?
I assure you that I can't . . . I mean, I haven't got any oil!

That sounds like an argument . . .
GOLDEN OIL

It's disgraceful, I tell you! Disgraceful!
GOLDEN OIL

Remember! On your own head be it!

OIL

AGENCY GOLDEN OIL

Tintin, let me introduce you to an old friend: Captain Chester, a shipmate of mine for more than twenty years.
I'm glad to hear it. I thought you were going to kill each other!

Gang of thieves! . . . Black marketeers! . . . Monopolizers! . . . Turncoats! . . . Ophicleides! . . . Colocynths!
Haddock!

Don't stop me! I'm going to exterminate those crooks! . . . The twisters!
Haddock, listen to me.
Calm down, Captain!

Listen to me. You're wasting your time. Do you know who's financed the "Peary" expedition? No? It was announced on the radio this morning. The Bohlwinkel Bank of São Rico.
So what? I don't mind! Blistering barnacles. I need fuel oil! . . .

All right, all right. D'you know who owns Golden Oil? . . . No? . . . The Bohlwinkel Bank, of São Rico. Now d'you understand?
?

Let me go! . . . I'm going to tear those caterpillars into little pieces!
Wait, Captain, I've got an idea!

An idea? About getting fuel oil?
Come on, we'll discuss this over a glass of whisky. Let's go into this bar.
Yes.

Barman! A bottle of whisky, and three glasses.
No whisky for me, thanks.
I'll have tonic water . . .
Two glasses, barman. And some tonic water for the lad.

By Jupiter, I've just remembered . . . I forgot you're the President of the Society of Sober Sailors. You don't drink whisky, of course. Tonic for you as well?
You're right . . . Tonic water . . . Good idea . . .

That's enough! . . . Thanks.

Here's to you, Haddock!
And to you! . . . Look, just to please you, I'll take a drop of whisky with my tonic . . . For old time's sake . . .

Only a drop . . . A thimbleful . . .

That's enough . . . Thanks!

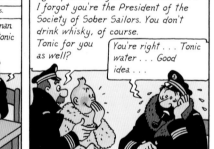

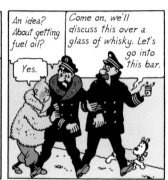

Aaaaaaaaah! . . . The tonic in these parts does you a power of good!

Now, tell us your idea.
Look, where is your ship moored?
Yes, where's she moored, the "Sisi" . . . the "Sirius"?

Just astern of the "Aurora".
That's fine! . . . And you're refuelling tomorrow morning? . . . Splendid! . . . Now, listen . . .
Li-li-listen carefully, Chester. This boy always has ex-x-x-x-cellent ideas.

The next morning . . .
GOLDEN OIL II

I say, Captain, d'you think there's a leak in your tanks? They don't seem to be filling.
OK, OK . . . They're big ones, that's all. Keep on pumping.
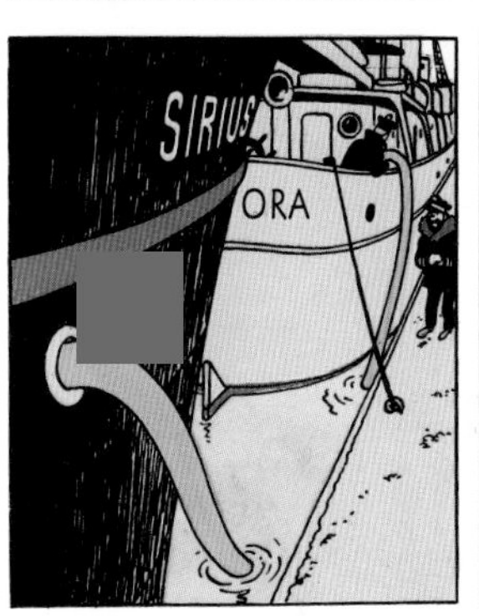
SIRIUS
ORA

That's the lot, Captain! Our tanks are full . . .

Will you send off this cable?
"Smithers, Golden Oil, Reykjavik. Your orders carried out. Aurora stays here until new instructions received. Signed: Payne." That'll be seven krónur.

TOOOOOT
ELEGRAPH

Good. That's the "Sirius" going out . . .

It's not the "Sirius"! . . . It's the "Aurora"!!

CRASH

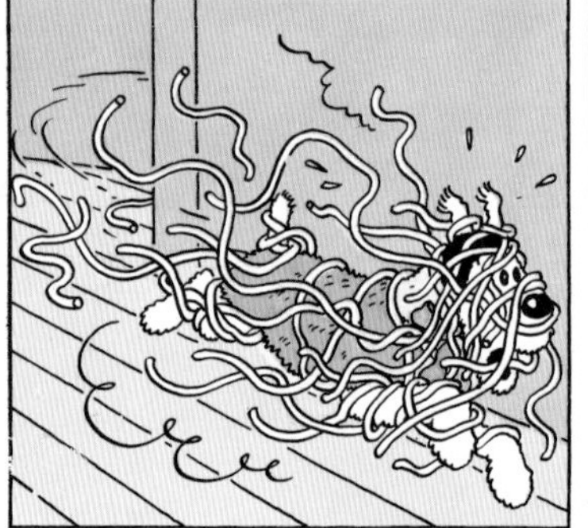

One must always keep one's sense of humour . . .

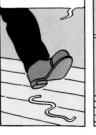

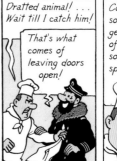

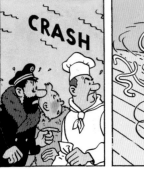

A week later . . .

This is where we are. We've crossed the 72nd parallel. You will confine your search to an area between 73 and 78 North, and 8 and 13 West . . . You understand?
Right.

Above all, don't take risks: don't go beyond the limits we fixed.

And don't forget to maintain contact by radio. Goodbye, and good luck. Keep your eyes skinned for the meteorite.
E.F.S.R.

AURORA

There they go . . .
Let's hope they don't run into any trouble.

Hello? . . . Hello? . . .
E.F.S.R.

Hello? . . . Receiving you loud and clear . . . What? . . . You've seen something?
The meteorite?

Something peculiar. The sky's quite clear. But there's a great column of white vapour rising from one spot about 20° East.

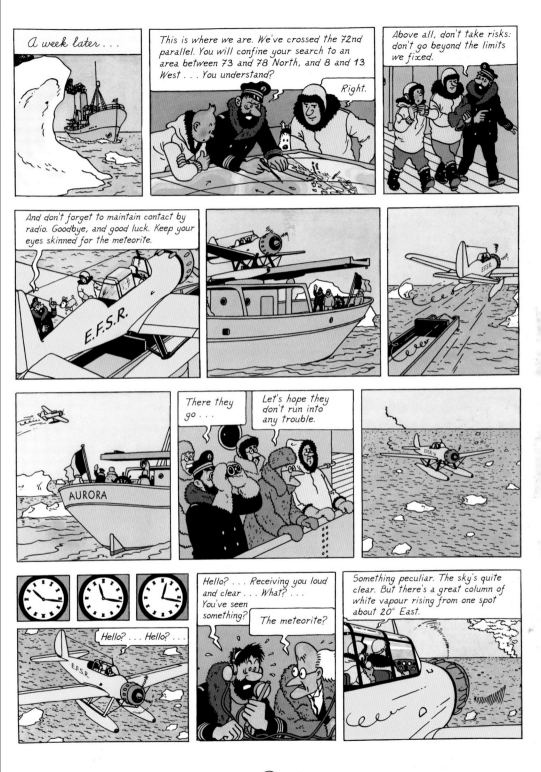

How extraordinary. They've seen a great column of white vapour on the horizon.
Quick! . . . Give me the microphone.

This is Professor Phostle. Tell me, does the column of vapour seem to be coming from a definite point? . . . You say there are no other clouds in sight? The sky is clear?

That's it! . . . They've found the meteorite!!
?

Careful! . . . The earphones . . .

Forgive me. I forgot! Yes, Captain, it's the meteorite causing the column of vapour. The heat emitted from it has already melted the ice. Gradually the water surrounding it is warming up.

Thus water-vapour is created, and this is rising up to form the clouds which they have seen.
Blistering barnacles!

Hello? Hello? . . . You have found the meteorite! . . . Hooray! . . . Hello? . . . Are you receiving me?

Hello? . . . Hello? . . . Hello? . . . They're not answering any more! . . .

Tell me, Captain, should these wires be connected to anything? . . .
Thundering typhoons! . . . The leads weren't plugged in!

There! That's fixed it.

Hello? . . . Ah, you can hear me . . . Turn round and come back . . . The vapour is caused by the meteorite . . . yes . . . Come back, you've completed your mission.

All right, we're returning.
E.F.S.R.

Look down there! . . .

Hello? . . . Yes? . . . What did you say? Smoke? . . . Smoke from a ship? . . . Where? . . . In which direction?

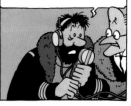

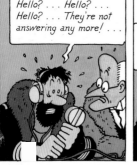

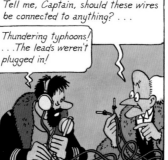

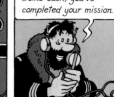

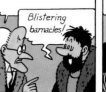

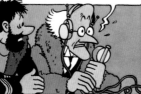

They're preparing to land . . . It'll be a miracle if they don't smash themselves up on an iceberg!

Well, Snowy old boy, if we get out of this in one piece we'll be lucky!

Thundering typhoons! . . . They scraped against that one . . . and that one too! . . . Whew! They just missed it!

We're done for this time, Snowy!
E.F.S.R.

E.F.S.R.

Hooray! He's a real ace!

E.F.S.R.

What news?
We haven't a moment to lose, Captain . . .
S.R.

The "Peary" is two hundred and fifty km ahead of us. We must overtake her!
Two hundred and fifty km ahead!!

E.F.S.R.
This is the end . . . We've lost the race.

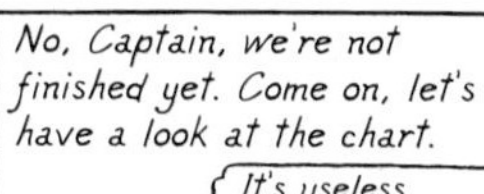
No, Captain, we're not finished yet. Come on, let's have a look at the chart.

It's useless.

Look, the "Peary" is there . . . And this is our position. Our maximum speed is 16 knots. The "Peary" can't do more than 12 knots. We could therefore gain on them by 6 km each hour. They're 250 km ahead. So in 37½ hours we'd have caught up with the "Peary" . . .
Yes, unless they'd reached the meteorite by then . . .
Captain, we must try to overtake the "Peary"! . . . This is no moment to throw up the sponge, just when victory is in sight.
Tintin's right; we must try, Captain.
That's all very fine! . . . But to catch up 250 km! . . .

Impossible! . . . It's quite futile to try. We're going to turn round and go home . . .

All right . . . er . . . I say, Captain, I'm frozen to death after that reconnaissance flight. I think I need a little whisky . . .
Some whisky? You? . . . er . . . I'll just see if there is any . . .

You'll have a glass with us, won't you, Captain?
You bet I will!

On second thoughts. I really do think the game is up. It'd be far better to give up the struggle . . .
!

Give up the struggle? . . . Never! . . . Blistering barnacles, this is no moment to throw up the sponge, just when victory is in sight! Thundering typhoons! . . . We'll show those P-P-Patagonian p-p-pirates what we can do! . . . The l-l-lily-livered l-l-landlubbers!

Come on! We shall see what we shall see! . . . Show a leg! On deck with you!

Get on with it, Chief! Thundering typhoons! jump to it! . . . Full speed ahead! The enemy have 250 km start on us: we've got to catch them up!

Cox'n at the wheel! Stick to your course. Steer North by East. And watch out for icebergs!
Aye, aye, sir.

Noon next day . . .
Hooray! . . . There she is! . . . That's smoke from the "Peary"!

We're steaming faster than she is! . . . We'll overtake them this evening, or during the night.

Captain! . . . A signal!

Read it! . . . This is the last straw! . . . What are we going to do? Blistering barnacles, what are we going to do?
!

Ask our scientists to come to the saloon. Tell them I have important news . . .

Gentlemen, I'd like to read you a signal we've just picked up. It's a distress call. The text is disjointed, as if the transmitter was damaged. Even the name of the ship is incomplete.

S.O.S. S.O.S. S.O.S.
CIT... 70°45' N.,
19° 12' W. IN
COLLISION WITH
ICEB... TAKING
WATER IN FORWA..
..QUEST
ASSISTANCE
URGE...

There it is, gentlemen. Either we can go to the aid of this ship, and abandon all hope of reaching the meteorite before the "Peary", or else we can continue on our course, and not answer this call . . . It's up to you to decide.

There's no question about it, Captain. Human lives are in danger. We must go to their aid, even if it does cost us our prize . . .
I was sure of your answer, Professor. We'll go about right away . . .
Bravo!

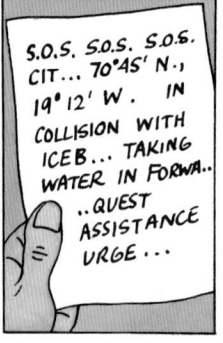

Come on. We must reply, and let them know we're coming to their assistance . . .
RADIO
?

I've forgotten to shut that confounded door again . . .

Polar research ship Aurora to Cit . . . in distress. Your message received. We are steaming towards you. Keep in touch with us. Good luck!

AURORA

Well?
That's the third time I've sent out the message . . . There's no reply.

I suppose their radio has packed up for good . . .
Yes, unless . . .

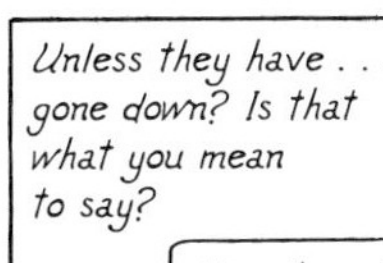
Unless they have . . . gone down? Is that what you mean to say?

No, it's not that . . .

Captain, will you let me send out a message myself?
Naturally, but . . .

?

Is that the text of what you want to send? It's absurd! What does the ship's name matter to us? . . . Anyway, you'll spend all night waiting for replies.
All night. Yes, I know.

You do as you like, but I think it's absolutely crazy. I'm going to turn in. Good night!
Good night, Captain . . . There. Could you send that off?
Right.

Polar research ship Aurora to all shipping companies. Please will all companies owning ships with name commencing "CIT" please advise us immediately of full names of these ships. Also inform us if one is in distress, position 70°45' N., 19°12' W.
AURORA

The next morning . . .
Good morning, boys! How goes it? Anyone answered your message?
RADIO

Is that all? . . . Well, what is the name of the ship in distress?
I still don't know! Here, look for yourself .

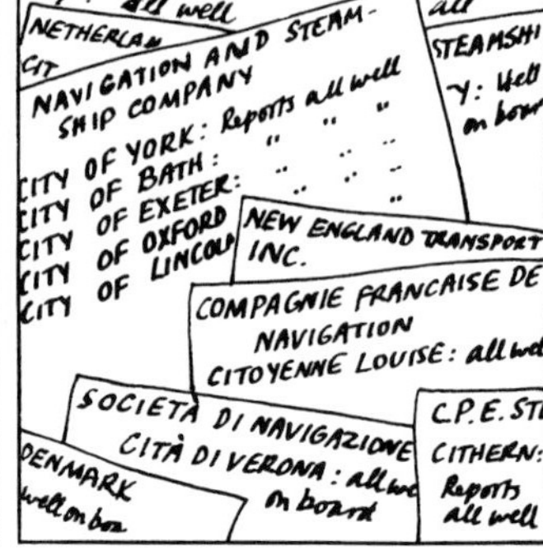

all well
NETHERLAN
CIT
NAVIGATION AND STEAM-SHIP COMPANY
CITY OF YORK: Reports all well
CITY OF BATH:
CITY OF EXETER:
CITY OF OXFORD
CITY OF LINCOLN
STEAMSHI
Y: Well on boar
all
NEW ENGLAND TRANSPORT INC.
COMPAGNIE FRANCAISE DE NAVIGATION
CITOYENNE LOUISE: all wel
SOCIETÀ DI NAVIGAZIONE CITÀ DI VERONA: all we on board
DENMARK well on boa
C.P.E. STE
CITHERN: Reports all well

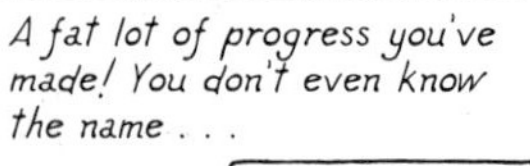

A fat lot of progress you've made! You don't even know the name . . .
Ssh! . . . There's another signal coming through.

Well?
We've got it. Here at last, the name of the ship. She's the "Cithara".

John Kingsby Navigation Company to Polar research ship Aurora. S.S. Cithara in distress 70°45' N., 19°12' W.

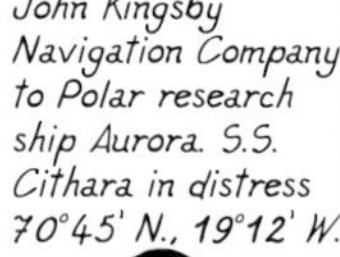

Now you've got what you want! There's your answer. She's the "Cithara" owned by the John Kingsby Company.

What are you looking for now? Her tonnage? Or her Captain's age? . . . Tell me, what more do you want to know?

Just one last detail, Captain. I think it will interest you. The "Cithara" does NOT exist!
!?

What do you mean? . . . Look here, that's impossible!
It's true, Captain! . . . The "Cithara" does not exist. Nor does the John Kingsby Navigation Company. The names don't appear in the register of shipping! Someone has sent us a fake S.O.S.!

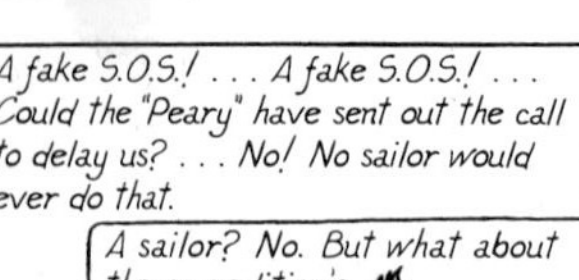

A fake S.O.S.! . . . A fake S.O.S.! . . . Could the "Peary" have sent out the call to delay us? . . . No! No sailor would ever do that.
A sailor? No. But what about the expedition's sponsors? . . .

Billions of blue blistering barnacles! Pirates! They'll need a distress signal when I get hold of them!

Here. Send out the following message: Polar research Ship Aurora to bogus John Kingsby Company . . . er . . . Deeply shocked by subterfuge . . . no . . . that's not strong enough . . . er . . . Gangsters! . . . that's it . . . Gangsters! Twisters! Traitors! . . . Woodlice! . . . Turncoats! . . . Ship-wreckers! . . . Mountebanks! Moujiks! Signed: Haddock.

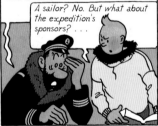

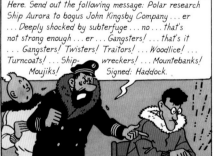

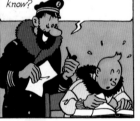

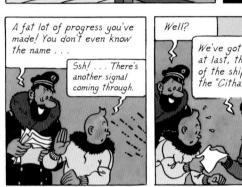

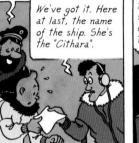

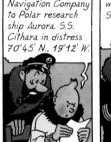

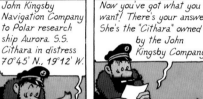

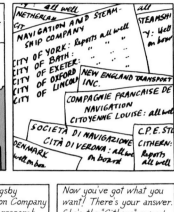

Quick, Captain, we must take up the chase!
And add: Rhizopods and Ectoplasms!

Helmsman ahoy! Wheel hard a starboard!

Hello, engine-room! . . . We're going after the "Peary" again. Increase your speed!
I wonder if we can possibly catch up with them . . .

Increase speed, Captain? . . . It's impossible . . . We're going all out already!

I don't care how you do it! . . . But we must go faster!

A fake S.O.S. . . . The pirates! . . . You know, if it hadn't been for you, we'd still be going south! . . . By the way, what first aroused your suspicions?

Thundering typhoons! What's the matter?

I think I must have fallen asleep . . .
It's true, you've been up all night. Go and get some sleep now.

You're right. I'll go to my cabin for an hour or so.
Have a good rest.

Snowy! . . . Come on, Snowy.

Whoever invented a ladder like this? You can see he never owned a dog!

Snowy? . . . Are you coming?

I'm too fagged out to undress. I'm asleep on my feet . . .
Still, you might remove my best bib and tucker.

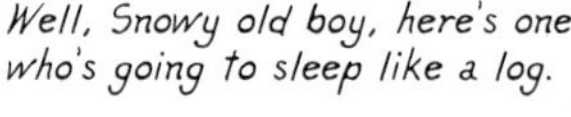

Well, Snowy old boy, here's one who's going to sleep like a log.

RAT
TAT
TAT
Yes?

It's me! Open up, quick! . . .
All right, coming . . .

Read this: it's a signal we've intercepted, from the "Peary".

R.S. Peary to Bohlwinkel, São Rico. Success. Meteorite in sight.

They've beaten us! . . . We're finished!

WOOAH!

No, we're not finished yet . . . The seaplane, Captain! Have the seaplane made ready . . .

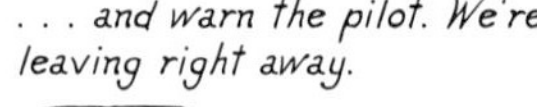

. . . and warn the pilot. We're leaving right away.
OK
Hey! What about our sleep?

Now, Snowy, you've got to stay here till I come back . . .

Don't be silly, Snowy; I'll soon be back.
E.F.S.R.

E.F.S.R.

WOW-OW-OW-OW-OW!
Come on, Snowy. He won't be long.

WOW-OW-OW-OW-OW-OW-OW-OW-OW!

Howling for the dead. A bad omen . . .

?

What is it now? . . . He's suddenly cheered up.

Blistering barnacles! The plane's returning . . .

Hello, he's landing . . . What can that mean?

The flag! . . . We forgot the flag to plant on the top of the meteorite.
Thundering typhoons! So we did . . .
E.F.S.R.

I'll go and fetch it.

There.
Thanks!

Off we go!
Snowy! . . . Here, Snowy! . . .
E.F.S.R.

Tintin! . . . Look out! . . . You've got Snowy!
E.F.S.R.

Oh Columbus! . . . They haven't seen him! Poor Snowy!
Oh my goodness!

E.F.S.R.

The radio! . . . We must warn them by radio! . . .

Hello? . . . Hello? . . . Hello? . . . Snowy's gone with you! . . . Yes, Snowy . . . He's clinging to the port wing of your aircraft.

!
!
E.F.

We must land.
No, we've no time to lose . . .
E

E.F.

E.F.

E

Hello? . . . Hello? . . . Snowy is safe! Yes, I've got him here with me . . .

We're getting near . . . There's the cloud of vapour rising from the meteorite . . .
E.F.S.R.

Some time later . . .
Hello, hello? . . . Captain Haddock here. Any news?
AURORA

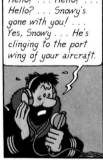

There isn't a single iceberg in sight, and the cloud of vapour is much nearer. We certainly can't be very far away now.
E.F.

The meteorite! There's the meteorite!

Hello . . . Tintin here . . . We can see the meteorite!!
Really? You mean that? . . . You can see the meteorite! . . . Hooray! . . . What's it like?

It forms an island, sloping gently towards the west, and . . . Great snakes! . . . The "Peary" has beaten us to it!

The "Peary" has beaten them to it.

Tell me . . . I suppose their flag is already flying from the top of the meteorite?

Their flag? . . . Wait . . . No, I can't see a flag . . .

Hooray! Then there's still hope!

Perhaps. I can just make out what's happening aboard the "Peary" . . . it looks as if . . . as if . . .
E.F.S.R.

Yes . . . they're just lowering a boat . . .

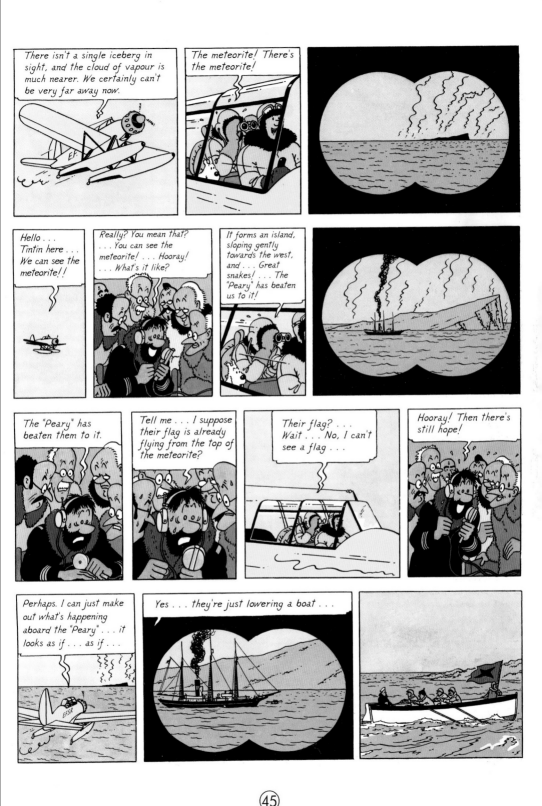

This is it! The meteorite is ours!
RRRRRRRRR
Hello! That sounds like an engine to me . . .
There, Captain, it's an aircraft!

It's the seaplane from the "Aurora", confound it!
Bah! By the time they've come down on the sea and launched their rubber dinghy, our men will be ashore on the meteorite.

E.F.S.R.
Anyway, it doesn't look as though they intend to land. They're simply flying over the meteorite.
Wooah!

Devil take it! He's jumped by parachute. He's going to land on the meteorite and plant his flag!

Crumbs! . . . The flag! . . .
That was lucky!
There he goes! He'll arrive before us!
No! I know how to stop him!

Faster! . . .
Faster! . . .

Pull! . . . Pull! . . .
Harder! . . . Harder! . . .
He'll get there before us!

Here comes the ground!

He'll get there before our lads. We're beaten!
Not yet . . .

?

What are you doing, Frank? Have you gone crazy?

Help! The wind has carried me too far!

?

Hooray! One more pull on the oars and we're there!

Quick! Quick!

I can't do it. The cord won't come undone . . .

Look! He's planted his flag!

E.F.S.R.

E.F.S.R.

Victory! Our flag is flying over the meteorite!

Victory!!

There he is, landing.

Snowy's coming to join you. He won't stay with me any longer.
Wooah!
Come on then, Snowy . . .
E.F.S.R.

?
Wooaaaaah!
E.F.S.R.

Snowy, my poor Snowy! . . . You must have banged against a rock!
Wooaaaaaaah!

OW! OWW! . . .

Ow! . . . Yow! . . . Yeow!
Wooaah!

The water's boiling! . . .
E.F.S.R.

Hello? . . . Hello? . . . Hello? . . .

Hello, I am receiving you . . . Yes . . . What? Serious . . . three days . . . Yes, of course. Good. Right . . .

The "Aurora" has developed engine trouble and has had to reduce speed. She won't be here for three days. We can't wait: we have no supplies. So we must get back and rejoin her. Anyway, our mission is accomplished. Are you coming?
E.F.S.R.

It's impossible. Someone must stay here to guard the island: that's only sense. So, what's to be done?

There's only one answer: I'll stay here and wait for you to come back with supplies. All right?
Tintin, you don't mean we're going to stay all by ourselves on this island?
E.F.S.R.

Right . . . I've got my emergency rations: a few biscuits, an apple and a flask of fresh water. I'll leave them with you.
E.F.S.R.

There . . .
Thanks.

Goodbye. And good luck. I'll be back in the morning.

There he goes.
I'll be glad when he's back!

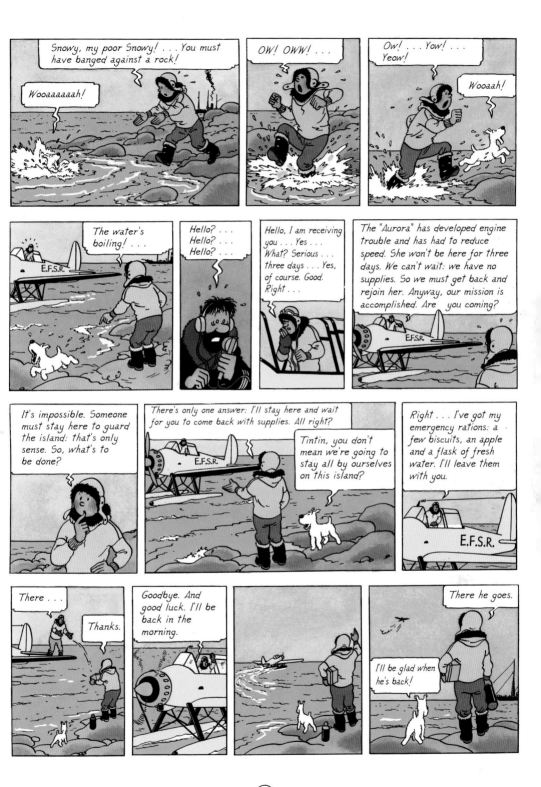

Now, Snowy, we'll have something to eat . . .
Good idea!

An apple, ship's biscuits and water: starvation, Snowy!
And how!

Starvation . . . that reminds me of Philippulus the prophet, with his predictions of hunger and cold!

And that nightmare when he was threatening me: "The judgement! . . . Yea! . . . Behold the judgement!"

And the judgement was an enormous spider. Brrr! I still go cold at the thought of it . . .

A spider!

Squash it, Tintin!

It's disappeared among the rocks.

Leave it. Come on, Snowy . . .

Enjoy your supper, Snowy. Let's forget that prophet of doom, with his spiders and his "dong-dong-dong".

DONG
DONG
DONG
!

What an ass I am. It's the bell on the "Peary".
DONG
DONG
DONG

It's their supper-time too, I expect . . .

Finished already, Snowy? I'm afraid I've nothing else for you. The two biscuits left are for tomorrow.

Golly! I'm still hungry! At least Tintin has an apple. If only I could find something to get my teeth into.

Ugh, there's a maggot in this apple . . .
Not a thing . . .

Whoops!

Are you coming, Snowy? We're going to turn in now. I'm absolutely dead beat.

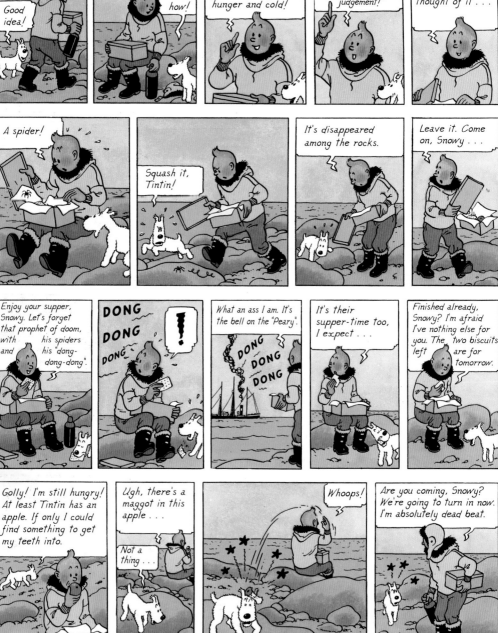

Our parachute will come in handy again. We can use it for a mattress and as a blanket.

Lucky for us the air is quite warm. It's extraordinary, when we're so near the Pole.

Good night, Snowy. Keep a good look out . . .

BOOM

?

I thought I heard an explosion . . . Hello, the "Peary" has disappeared. She must have weighed anchor while we were asleep.

Still, that explosion? . . . I suppose I was dreaming . . .

BOOM

!
Tintin, I'm s . . . s . . . scared!

I've got it! It must be the island itself. It's probably a kind of small volcano . . . or a volcanic vent of some sort.

No! Not a sign of a crack, nor of a crater . . . So, now what?

!
Wooah! Wooah!

Snowy's found something: he looks pleased with himself!

An egg! . . . A egg!! . . . Great snakes! . . . Who can have laid that?
Come on, Tintin, let's scramble it.

But . . . but . . . Unless I'm seeing things . . . The egg: it's getting bigger!

It's not an egg! It's a mushroom! . . .

BOOM

The mushroom . . . vaporised, vanished into thin air!

BOOM
BOOM
BOOM

BOOM
BOOM

Things seem to be calming down a bit . . .
BOOM

Yes, it's over. Whew! If that's the effect of the new metal, we're in for some more surprises!

Ssh! . . .

No, nothing. The sky is empty . . .

I thought I heard a buzzing, like the noise of an engine . . .

!

An apple tree! . . . Good heavens, it's an apple tree! . . . It must have been the core I threw away yesterday . . . It's incredible! . . . Fantastic! . . .
I'm keeping an eye open in case the tree blows up too.

It must be magic!

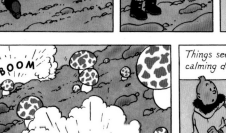

!
WOOAAAH!

Shoo!! . . . Get away, you horrible creature!

Where did that huge insect come from? It can't be . . . Yes, it must have been from the maggot I found in the apple!

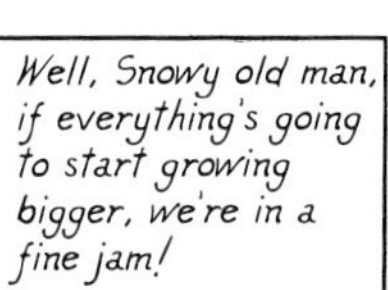
Well, Snowy old man, if everything's going to start growing bigger, we're in a fine jam!

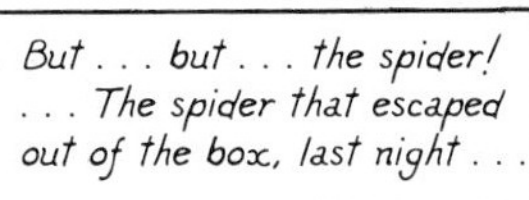
But . . . but . . . the spider! . . . The spider that escaped out of the box, last night . . .

I say, Tintin you don't think that will have grown, too?

If it's still alive it should be near the apple tree: that's where I was sitting yesterday.

Careful! . . . It might appear at any moment . . .

?
THUMP

Great snakes!
THUMP

?
?

An earthquake! That's the last straw!

And what's that rumbling?

Help! That huge wave will swamp everything!

Whew! . . . Safe! The water isn't coming up any further.

I say, the whole island has tilted right over.

In the meantime more apple trees have sprung up.
Hey, what about the spider?
Ssh! . . . Quiet! . . .

This time I'm sure of it . . . I can hear the sound of an engine.

There Snowy! . . . The seaplane . . .
Hooray! . . . We're saved!

Oh, what a beautiful mo-o-orming!

Oh, what a tra-la la-la!
!

Tra-la-la-la-la-la-la-a-a-la

Everything's going my way!

Crumbs! What a monster!

If only I can grab a stone . . .

Got one! . . . And it hasn't budged . . .

Now, take a good aim . . .

Missed it!

Great snakes! another earthquake!

!

Whew! That was close! Thank goodness for the apple tree!

Hello? Hello? . . . The meteorite has just been shaken by an earthquake. The whole thing has tilted over, and is sinking slowly into the sea.

What did you say? . . . An earthquake? . . . The meteorite is sinking? . . . What about Tintin? Where is he?
We're losing the meteorite?

Can't see him . . . Oh, yes . . . He's lying at the foot of an enormous tree, quite still. The water will soon reach him.
E.F.S.R.

Try to land! . . . Tintin must be saved!

Impossible to get down, Captain. The sea's absolutely raging!
E.F.S.R.

Tintin! . . . Tintin! . . . Wake up!

Not a flicker. And the water's still rising! . . . What can I do?

WOOAH! . . . WOOAH! . . .
It's no good! . . . But he simply must come round!

OWW!

What's got into you, Snowy? Why did you bite me?
Quick, we must get a move on!

Now what's happening? . . . Great snakes! The meteorite's tipping over!

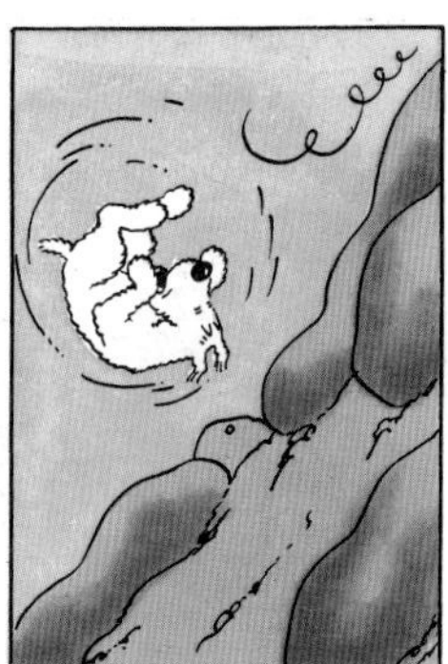

Quick, up to the top. The island is settling more and more . . .

Here goes! It's neck or nothing! I simply must save him!
E.F.S.R.

E.F.S.R.

What's he doing? . . . Is he going to land? . . . It's sheer lunacy!

I can't see him any more. I hope to heaven he hasn't crashed . . .

He made it! He managed to get down safely!

Now he's hidden by the waves again . . .

Hooray! He's succeeded in launching the rubber dinghy.

I can't come any closer: I'd be dashed on the rocks. I'll throw you a line with a life-jacket attached. Haul in the line and put the life-jacket on.
Right!

Here quickly, Snowy. We'll try to reach the dinghy . . .
Jump in? . . . Me? Never again!

Snowy! . . . Snowy! . . . Come on, come here at once!

I don't want to go in the water! . . . Wow! . . . Wow!

All right, stop crying. You aren't going in the water.

I'll throw you! Catch!

One . . . two . . .

No, he might fall in the sea. I'll try another way.

Come on, Snowy, get in!
?

That's Snowy safe! Now it's my turn. But first . . .

. . . I'll replace the flag. It must fly over the meteorite to the end.

E.F.S.R.

I'll throw you the rope, and you can haul me across.
Right!

Here goes!

Got you!

Safe at last!
Now, let's get out of here, fast!

What an idiot I am!

?

What are you doing? It's madness to go back!

For heaven's sake come back! You'll go down with the meteorite!

We must have a lump of the mineral . . . for Professor Phostle. Otherwise all our efforts will have been wasted!

Quick! . . . Catch!

Tintin! . . . I can't see Tintin!

No sign of Tintin . . .

Yes, there, hanging on to the lump of phostlite . . . with the flag, too!

Meanwhile . . .
Nothing . . . not a word . . . What's become of them?

It's them! . . . I've got them! . . . Hello? . . . Hello? . . .
The seaplane?

Hello? . . . Yes . . . Yes . . . Yes . . . Good!
The meteorite? What of the meteorite?

They're returning! . . . They're safe and sound! . . . Hooray!

Some hours later . . .
There they are! There they are!

E.F.S.R.

Here you are, I've brought you a lump of phostlite . . . wrapped in the expedition's flag.
E.F

?
E

Some weeks later . . .

The polar research ship "Aurora", which sailed in search of the meteorite that fell in the Arctic, will soon be back in home waters. The expedition succeeded in finding the meteorite, just before it was submerged by the waves – probably as a result of some underwater upheaval. Happily, thanks to the courage and presence of mind shown by the young reporter Tintin, alone on the island at the very moment . . .

. . . when it was engulfed by the sea, it was possible to save a lump of the metal divined in the meteorite by Professor Phostle. Members of the expedition have already verified the remarkable properties of the metal; examination of it will undoubtedly be of extraordinary scientific interest. We may therefore look forward to more sensational disclosures.

It is now known that certain incidents that occurred during the voyage of the "Aurora" were unquestionably deliberate acts of sabotage designed to cripple the expedition. Those responsible will soon be exposed, and their leader unmasked. This master criminal is reported to be a powerful São Rico financier. He will shortly be brought to justice.

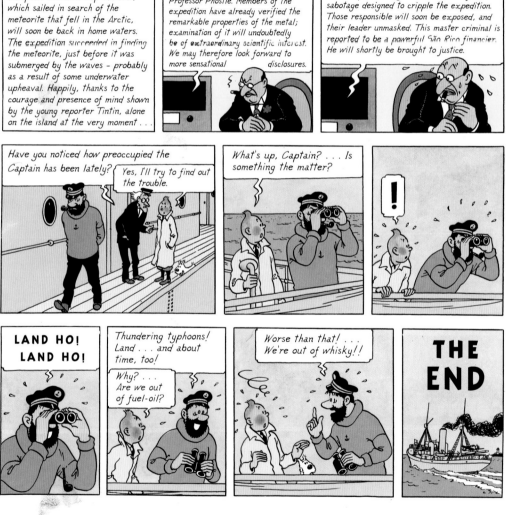

THE REAL-LIFE INSPIRATION BEHIND TINTIN'S ADVENTURES

Written by Stuart Tett
with the collaboration of Studio Moulinsart.

1907	1924	1925	1928	1929
GEORGES REMI BORN IN BELGIUM	CHOOSES PEN-NAME "HERGÉ"—HIS INITIALS "G.R." REVERSED	HERGÉ LEAVES SCHOOL	HERGÉ HELPS TO CREATE CHILDREN'S MAGAZINE *LE PETIT VINGTIÈME*	TINTIN'S FIRST ADVENTURE, *TINTIN IN THE LAND OF THE SOVIETS*, APPEARS IN *LE PETIT VINGTIÈME*

Discover something new and exciting

HERGÉ

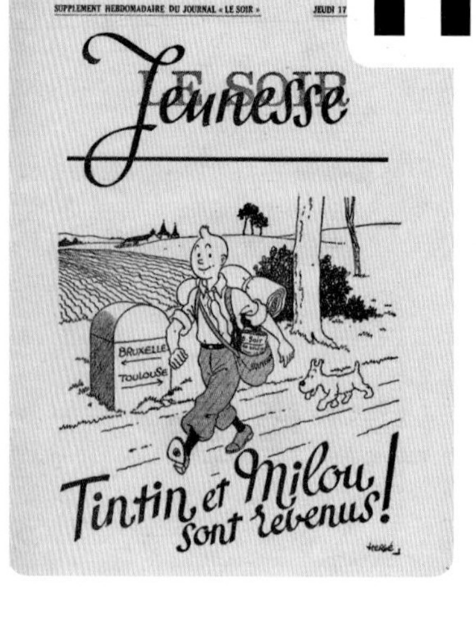

SUPPLEMENT HEBDOMADAIRE DU JOURNAL « LE SOIR » JEUDI 17

LE SOIR Jeunesse

Tintin et Milou sont revenus!

HERGÉ

Le Soir Jeunesse

Le Petit Vingtième magazine was closed down during World War II. Hergé began publishing Tintin in *Le Soir Jeunesse*, a new children's magazine that came with copies of *Le Soir* newspaper. Below you can see an illustration that Hergé created for one of the magazine columns. *Actualités* means "news" in French.

1942	1946	1971	1976	1983
PUBLICATION OF *THE SHOOTING STAR*	LAUNCH OF *TINTIN* MAGAZINE	HERGÉ VISITS AMERICA	PUBLICATION OF TINTIN'S LAST ADVENTURE, *TINTIN AND THE PICAROS*	HERGÉ DIES AGED 75

about Tintin and his creator Hergé!

TINTIN

Practical science

Tintin is a bit like a detective, but there is also something of a scientist about him. Although he may not have a laboratory, he loves to use everyday objects for his off-the-cuff experiments. Unfortunately, Snowy doesn't always understand his master's flashes of inspiration.

THE TRUE STORY
...behind *The Shooting Star*

Tintin looks up into the beautiful, starry sky during a night-time stroll. He stops in amazement: there seems to be one star too many in the Great Bear! In astronomy (the study of stars, planets and other objects in the sky), the Great Bear is a constellation—an area of the sky marked by certain stars. Tintin tries to point out the strange extra star to Snowy, but since Snowy's just walked into a lamp post, he's too busy seeing stars of his own!

The circled star is named μ UMa (the Greek letter μ is pronounced "mu"; UMa is short for the Great Bear's Latin name, Ursa Major). Find out more about this star on page 16.

Once upon a time…

The origins of astronomy can be traced back over 5,000 years; the earliest star catalogues date from around 1200 B.C. Many centuries later, a Roman mathematician and astronomer named Claudius Ptolemy (90–168 A.D.) created a star catalogue listing 1,022 stars in 48 constellations. Many of Ptolemy's constellation names are still in use today—including the Great Bear! The seven brightest stars of the Great Bear make up a pattern commonly known in America as the Big Dipper (shown with yellow lines above).

In the Young Readers edition of *Tintin in America* you can read about Hergé's childhood, when he was part of a scout troop. Learning about the star constellations is just the kind of thing he might have done on a scout camping trip.

The observatory

Sensing a mystery, Tintin telephones the observatory to find out more about the strange, bright star. Dissatisfied with the curt reply he receives, Tintin sets off to visit the observatory in person.

Once upon a time...

From as early as the late 1920s, Hergé made regular visits to the Royal Observatory of Belgium, in Brussels. Hergé spoke with numerous astronomers at the observatory. He would ask their advice, and they would check the astronomical science in his stories to make sure that he got it right!

Eugène Delporte (1882–1955) was a Belgian astronomer. In 1930 Delporte defined precisely the modern boundaries between the star constellations. He searched the skies for asteroids, discovering sixty-six in total. In 1936 he became director of the Royal Observatory.

Sylvain Arend (1902–1992) enjoyed discussing astronomy with Hergé. In January 1931, astronomers were excited about the close position of asteroid 433 Eros to Earth. Perhaps discussing the asteroid's trajectory with Arend gave Hergé his first ideas for *The Shooting Star*? In 1953, Sylvain Arend discovered a new asteroid, which was later named 1652 Hergé, after his friend!

Observation dome,
The Royal Observatory of Belgium

Comets and shooting stars

In 1880, members of the observatory in Brussels founded *Ciel et Terre* (meaning "Sky and Earth") astronomy magazine. In the 1930s and 1940s, Sylvain Arend, Eugène Delporte and many others wrote articles about comets and meteors—bits of asteroids that burn up in Earth's atmosphere, commonly known as shooting stars—for *Ciel et Terre*.

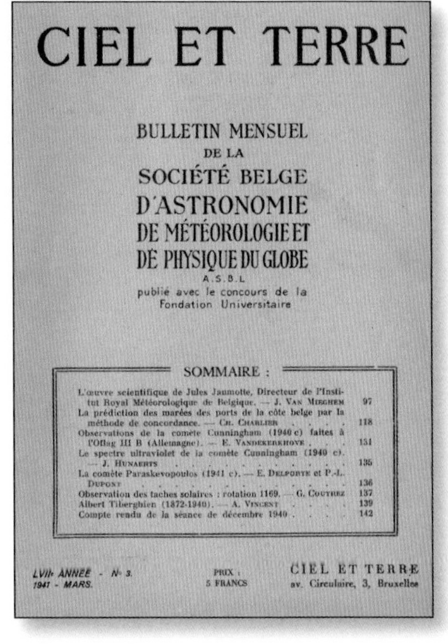

CIEL ET TERRE

BULLETIN MENSUEL
DE LA
SOCIÉTÉ BELGE
D'ASTRONOMIE
DE MÉTÉOROLOGIE ET
DE PHYSIQUE DU GLOBE
A.S.B.L
publié avec le concours de la Fondation Universitaire

SOMMAIRE :

L'œuvre scientifique de Jules Jaumotte, Directeur de l'Institut Royal Météorologique de Belgique. — J. Van Mieghem	97
La prédiction des marées des ports de la côte belge par la méthode de concordance. — Ch. Charlier	118
Observations de la comète Cunningham (1940 c) faites à l'Oflag III B (Allemagne). — E. Vandekerkhove	131
Le spectre ultraviolet de la comète Cunningham (1940 c). — J. Hunaerts	135
La comète Paraskevopoulos (1941 c). — E. Delporte et P.-L. Dupont	136
Observation des taches solaires : rotation 1169. — G. Coutrez	137
Albert Tiberghien (1872-1940). — A. Vincent	139
Compte rendu de la séance de décembre 1940	142

LVIIe ANNÉE - N° 3.
1941 - MARS.
PRIX : 5 FRANCS
CIEL ET TERRE
av. Circulaire, 3, Bruxelles

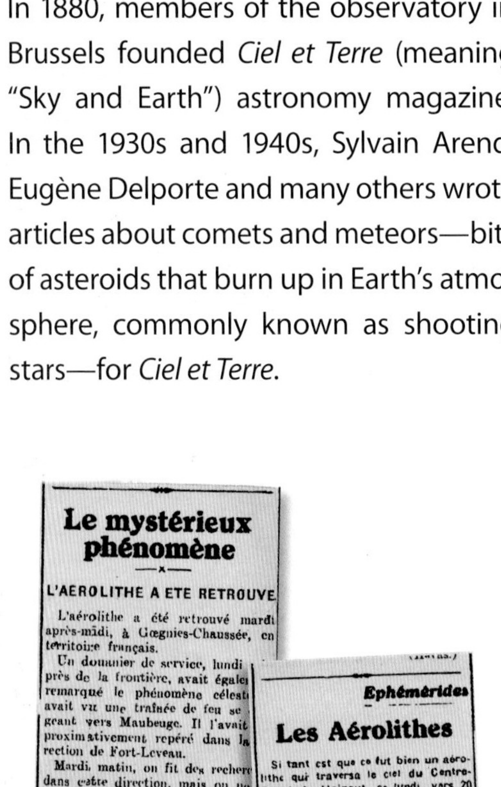

Le mystérieux phénomène

L'AEROLITHE A ETE RETROUVE

L'aérolithe a été retrouvé mardi après-midi, à Gœgnies-Chaussée, en territoire français.

Un douanier de service, lundi près de la frontière, avait égale remarqué le phénomène célest avait vu une traînée de feu se geant vers Maubeuge. Il l'avait proximativement repéré dans la rection de Fort-Leveau.

Mardi, matin, on fit des recher dans cette direction, mais on ne trouva rien.

Cependant, un cultivateur habit le hameau de Maubarson, à Gœgni Chaussée, en se rendant sur champ, labouré la veille, constata le terrain était complètement, vaillé et qu'une traînée se termin par un trou, extrêmement profon s'avançant de biais dans le sol.

Le cultivateur, M. Caminade, ne doutant pas qu'il pût s'agir d'un a rolithe, reboucha le trou. Mais rentrant chez lui, il raconta ce qu' avait constaté et on se rendit sur le lieux indiqués.

On creusa le sol et, au fond d trou, on constata la présence d'u aérolithe, large d'environ 35 centim tres et long d'en

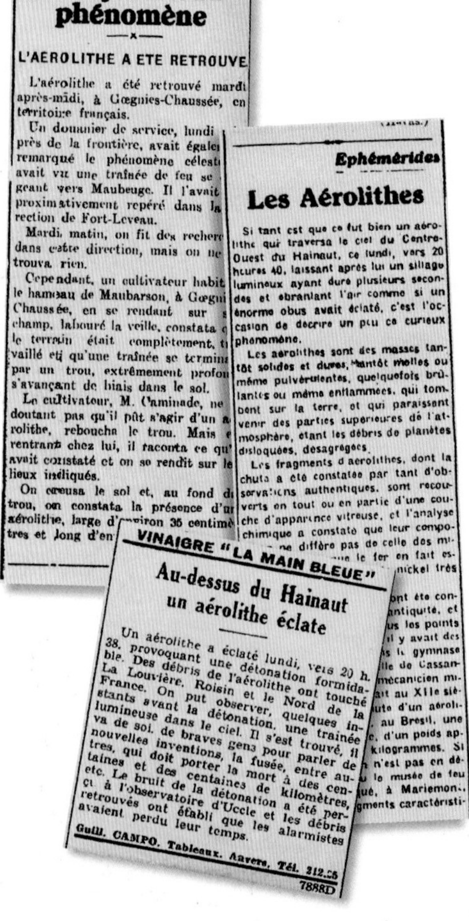

Ephémérides

Les Aérolithes

Si tant est que ce fut bien un aérolithe qui traversa le ciel du Centre-Ouest du Hainaut, ce lundi, vers 20 heures 40, laissant après lui un sillage lumineux ayant duré plusieurs secondes et ébranlant l'air comme si un énorme obus avait éclaté, c'est l'occasion de décrire un peu ce curieux phénomène.

Les aérolithes sont des masses tantôt solides et dures, tantôt molles ou même pulvérulentes, quelquefois brûlantes ou même enflammées, qui tombent sur la terre, et qui paraissent venir des parties supérieures de l'atmosphère, étant les débris de planètes disloquées, désagrégées.

Les fragments d'aérolithes, dont la chute a été constatée par tant d'observations authentiques, sont recouverts en tout ou en partie d'une couche d'apparence vitreuse, et l'analyse chimique a constaté que leur composition ne diffère pas de celle des mi... le fer en fait es... nickel très ...ont été con... antiquité, et ...us les points ...il y avait des ...s l... gymnase ...le de Cassan... mécanicien mi... ...it au XIIe siè... ...ute d'un aéroli... au Brésil, une ...c, d'un poids ap... kilogrammes. Si ...n'est pas en dé... le musée de feu ...ué, à Mariemon... ...gments caractéristi...

VINAIGRE "LA MAIN BLEUE"

Au-dessus du Hainaut un aérolithe éclate

Un aérolithe a éclaté lundi, vers 20 h. 38, provoquant une détonation formidable. Des débris de l'aérolithe ont touché La Louvière, Roisin et le Nord de la France. On put observer, quelques instants avant la détonation, une traînée lumineuse dans le ciel. Il s'est trouvé, il va de soi, de braves gens pour parler de nouvelles inventions, la fusée, entre autres, qui doit porter la mort à des centaines et des centaines de kilomètres, etc. Le bruit de la détonation a été perçu à l'observatoire d'Uccle et les débris retrouvés ont établi que les alarmistes avaient perdu leur temps.

Guil. CAMPO. Tableaux. Anvers. Tél. 312.25
7888D

Once upon a time...

Meteors travel dozens of times faster than jet aeroplanes! At these speeds rubbing against the air in the atmosphere creates so much force (called friction) that the space rocks begin to burn. On November 25, 1934, a meteor blew up over the southern Belgian province of Hainaut, scattering fragments around the border with France. The explosion was registered at the Royal Observatory in Brussels, 50 miles away. Belgian newspapers reported the story, and there were also several articles about it in *Ciel et Terre*.

Incoming fireball!

Professor Phostle may have no trouble explaining precisely how bad things are, but Tintin can't bear to imagine it: a huge ball of fire is heading straight for Earth! They use a giant telescope to examine the immense asteroid. Although the real telescope in use at the time at the Royal Observatory of Belgium was of the same design, it was much smaller.

The telescope Hergé drew is much more like the one on the next page. Let's **Explore and Discover!**

EXPLORE AND DISCOVER

- ★ This giant telescope is housed at the Yerkes Observatory in the USA.
- ★ It was built in the 1890s and became fully operational in 1897.
- ★ The telescope is a *refractor*—it uses a lens to gather and focus light. *Reflector* telescopes use a series of mirrors to do the same task.
- ★ The telescope's 40-inch-wide lens made it the largest usable refractor telescope in the world when it was built...and it still is today!
- ★ Hergé would have heard about a Belgian astronomer called Georges Van Biesbroeck (1880–1974), a specialist in double stars, asteroids and comets. In 1916, Van Biesbroeck left his job at the Royal Observatory of Belgium for a position at the Yerkes Observatory.
- ★ In 1935, Sylvain Arend, Hergé's friend at the Royal Observatory, travelled to Yerkes himself to further his own research on double stars.

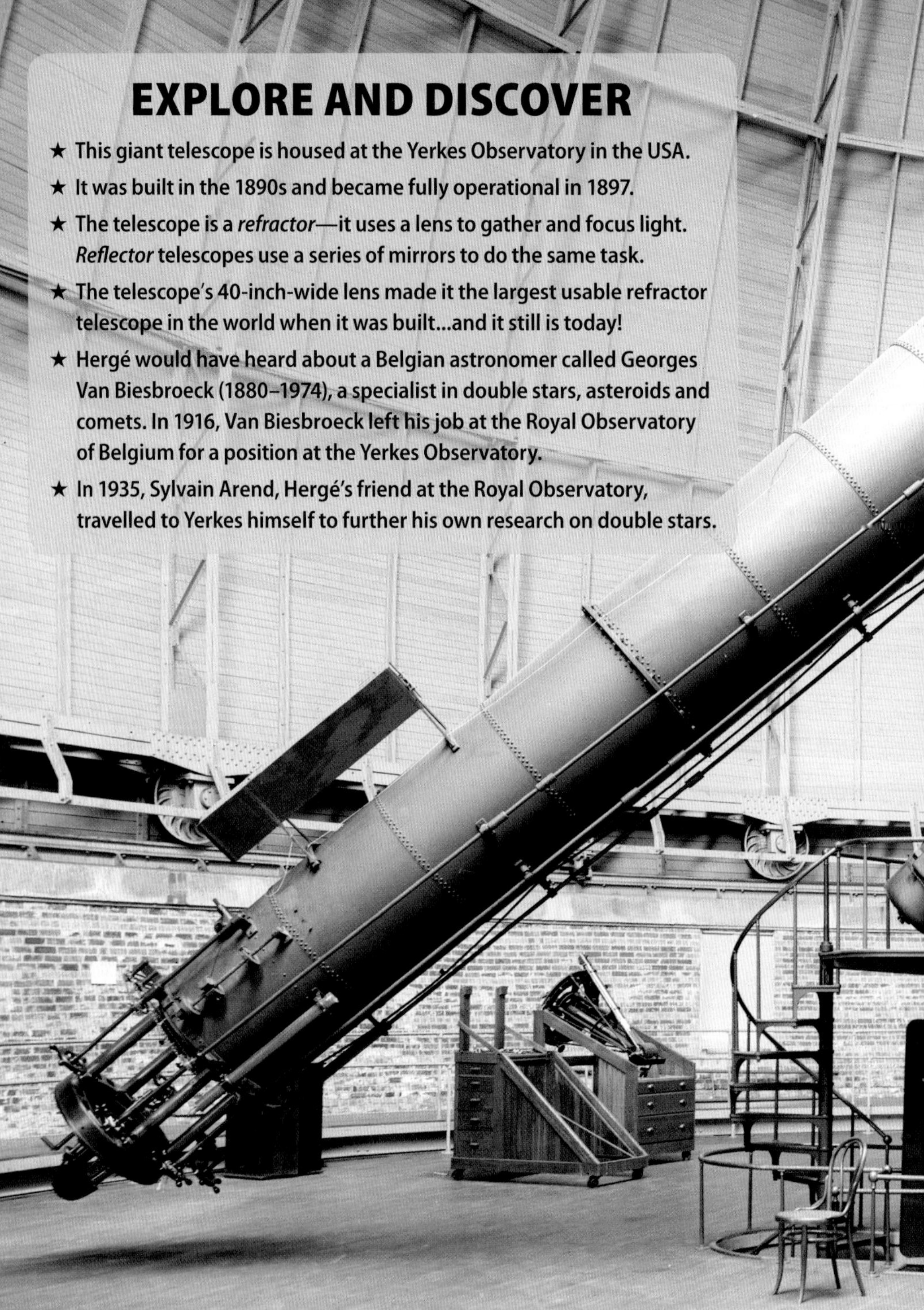

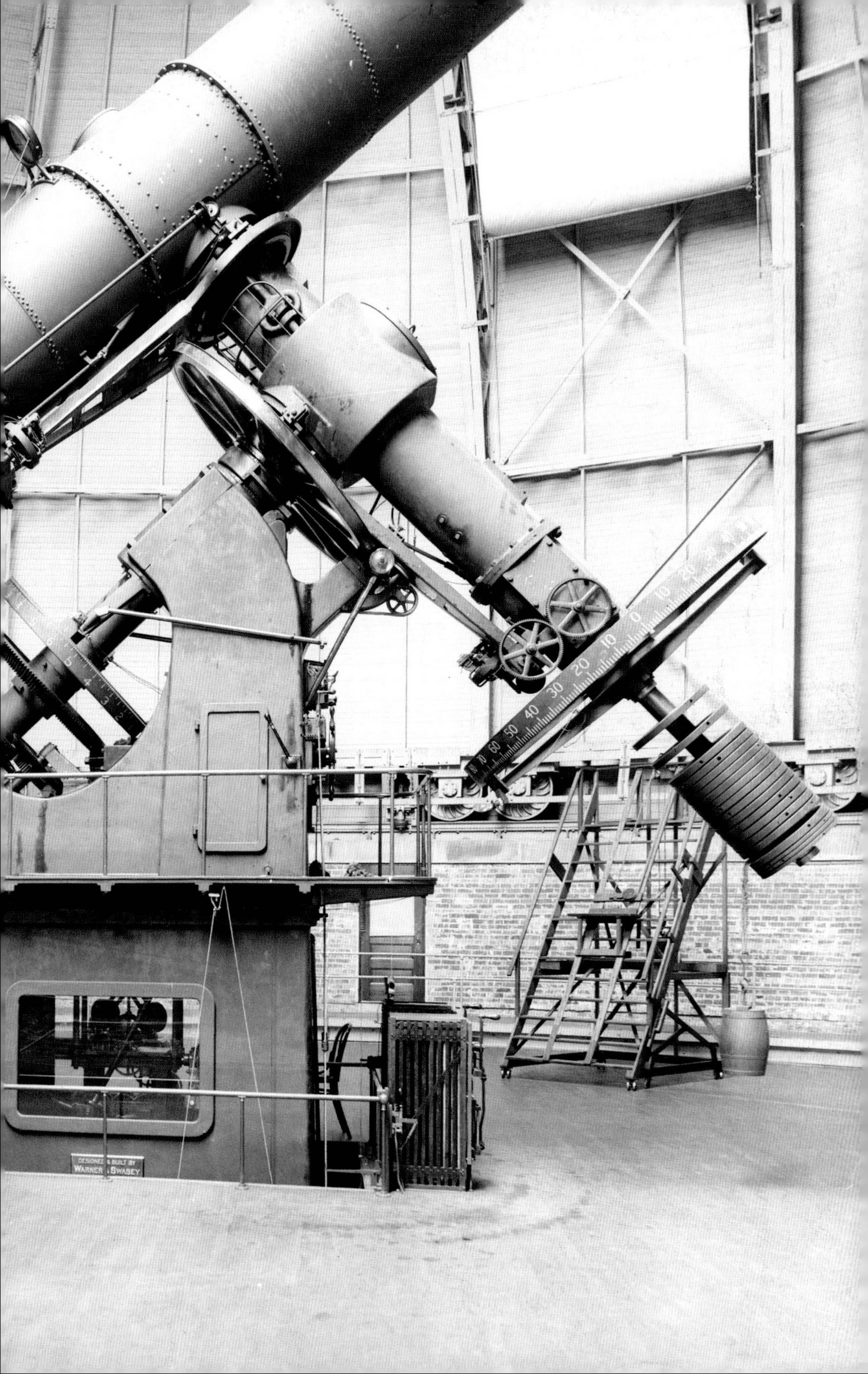
DESIGNED & BUILT BY
WARNER & SWASEY

COUNTDOWN TO THE END OF THE WORLD

Professor Phostle's assistant has completed his complex mathematical calculations. The end of the world is scheduled for the next morning! It's tempting to think that Hergé based this character on a real person. Check out the photo of Henri Poincaré (1854–1912), a French mathematician who some people credit with discovering the theory of relativity before Albert Einstein (1879–1955). Does Poincaré look like the mathematician in the story?

PROPHET OF DOOM

One of the scientists from the observatory can't take it anymore. He goes home and transforms himself into… Philippulus the prophet! Things were looking bad enough, and now Tintin has to put up with all that gong-banging!

METEORITES

Meteorites are meteors—chunks of asteroids or sometimes bit of comets—that do not fully burn up in Earth's atmosphere, and instead crash into Earth.

★ Most meteorites are one of three kinds: chondrites (stony), iron meteorites (made mostly of iron and nickel) or carbonaceous chondrites (contain organic compounds).

★ Below is a picture of the Barringer Crater near Winslow, Arizona. It was formed around 50,000 years ago by an iron meteorite around 150 feet across and weighing several hundred thousand tons. The crater is 550 feet deep and 4,100 feet across.

★ Meteorites around a mile wide collide with Earth around every million years.

★ Many scientists believe that dinosaurs were wiped out by the effects of the huge meteorite strike that created the 110-mile-wide Chicxulub crater on the coastline of Mexico around 65 million years ago (the crater is now underground). The meteorite was around seven miles wide and devastated an immense area, as well as causing dust to cover the entire planet, creating a deadly environment for most living things. Such catastrophic events are extremely rare!

Luckily for Tintin, the people of Brussels and the whole world, the professor's assistant got his calculations wrong! The asteroid passes by Earth, missing it by 48,000 km (30,000 miles—an eighth of the distance from Earth to the Moon). But there is an earthquake caused by a piece of the asteroid falling into the Arctic Ocean.

POLAR EXPEDITIONS

In the story, a piece of the huge asteroid that brushes past Earth falls into the Arctic Ocean.

★ In 1969, a group of Japanese scientists travelled to the Antarctic (on the opposite side of the world from the Arctic, but just as cold) and discovered a meteorite.

★ The study of meteorites and the substances that they are made of is an extremely useful way of learning about the powerful processes that led to the creation of the solar system.

★ Tests indicated that the Antarctic meteorite was more than 4.5 billion years old and that it came from an asteroid orbiting between Mars and Jupiter.

★ But the most exciting discovery came when scientists found traces of an unknown mineral in the meteorite—a mineral not found on Earth.

★ Out of respect for a certain Professor John Wasson, a specialist in the study of meteorites, the new mineral discovered in the Antarctic meteorite was named wassonite!

Artwork by Mark Elwood, 2011

PHOSTLITE

I, Decimus Phostle, have discovered a new metal! I shall give my name to it: phostlite.
My heartiest congratulations!

Professor Phostle has discovered a new metal in the meteorite and he wastes no time in naming it phostlite...after himself! But the professor did not have a sample of the meteorite to study. He learned about the new metal by using a spectroscopic photograph of the shooting star taken through his telescope.

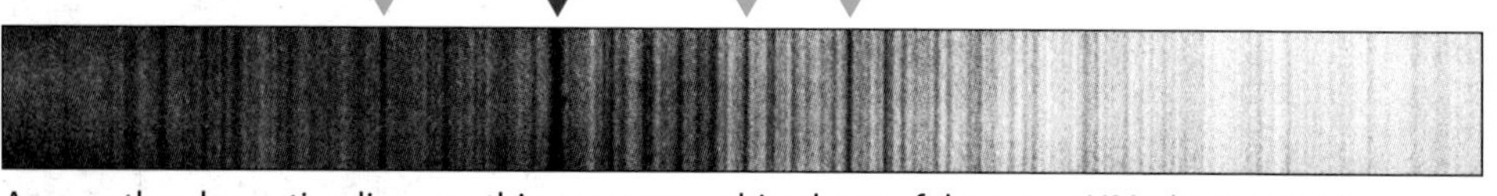

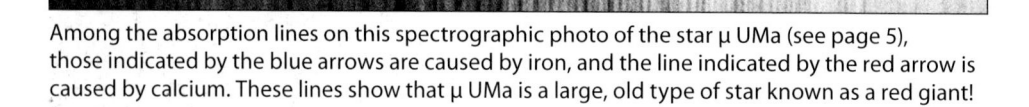

Among the absorption lines on this spectrographic photo of the star μ UMa (see page 5), those indicated by the blue arrows are caused by iron, and the line indicated by the red arrow is caused by calcium. These lines show that μ UMa is a large, old type of star known as a red giant!

SPECTROSCOPE

The word "spectrum" can refer to the bands of different colours—wavelengths of light—seen when visible light is split using a prism or spectroscope. In general, stars emit a continuous spectrum of visible light (the entire range of wavelengths) as well as radiation at wavelengths beyond the visible range. But chemical elements in the outer layers of stars actually absorb particular wavelengths of light. This absorption shows up in a spectrum as dark lines—absorption lines. Sometimes certain chemical elements emit wavelengths of light that show up in a spectrum as bright lines called emission lines. Studying all these lines can help scientists to deduce many things about stars, including which chemical elements are present inside them, how hot they are and how fast they are travelling!

PROFESSOR PHOSTLE

Professor Phostle is extremely passionate about astronomy, so passionate that he is fearless. The professor loses his temper when he discovers that his colleague's calculations are mistaken and the world is not going to end!

PASSIONATE SCIENTISTS

- ★ **The Belgian astronomer Georges Van Biesbroeck (see page 10) was once in hospital following a serious accident.**
- ★ **A visiting student, not knowing what to say to such an ill man, blurted out, "Mr. Van B, this evening I observed Comet Tago-Sato-Kosaka!"**
- ★ **Reportedly, Van Biesbroeck's eye popped open and he said, "Did you notice that its nucleus has split in three?"**

You have already learned about some of the real scientists Hergé met at the Royal Observatory of Belgium, but there was another one you haven't heard of, named Edgard Vandekerkhove (1902–1978). The funny thing is, Vandekerkhove liked to give treats to people visiting the observatory, just like Professor Phostle!

Go out and buy ten penny-worth of bull's eyes! We must have a fitting celebration of my discovery!

THE *AURORA*

Setting off to find the meteorite, Professor Phostle leads a team of scientists to the Arctic Ocean. Tintin helps to organise the expedition, while Captain Haddock commands the ship used by the scientists: the *Aurora*.

When interviewed later in his life, Hergé said that he was not happy with the *Aurora*, and that she would have sunk—not because of the dangerous icebergs in the Arctic Ocean, but because of the way he drew the ship. Despite the great lengths Hergé went to when creating the *Aurora*, experts told him that the design was not correct!

ARCHIVE PHOTOS

Hergé based some panels on photographs. The photo below shows a ship's engineer at work, and the corresponding panel may bring to mind a popular *Star Trek* character. In nearly every *Star Trek* television episode or film there is a scene when Scotty, the engineer of the starship *Enterprise*, receives emergency instructions in the engine room to speed up the spaceship, to which he replies, "I'm giving her all she's got, captain!"

THERE IS ONLY ONE THING FOR IT... THE SEAPLANE!

The rival expedition trying to reach the meteorite has pulled ahead by sending a phoney SOS—a distress signal—to distract Tintin and his team. Captain Haddock thinks they have been beaten, but suddenly Tintin has an idea!

ARADO AR 196

★ The Arado Ar 196 was a German two-seater reconnaissance seaplane.

★ The aircraft was launched from a catapult extended over the side of a ship. To return, the plane landed in the water next to its ship and was hoisted on board using a crane.

★ The Arado Ar 196 had a wingspan of 40.5 feet, and it was 36 feet long and 14.5 feet tall. It weighed 6,600 pounds when empty. It could reach a top speed of 193 mph and fly to a maximum height of 22,960 feet.

★ Although over 500 of these aircraft were manufactured, today only two or three survive in museums.

With no time to lose, the pilot of the seaplane takes to the skies...with Tintin riding in the back seat! As they fly over the meteorite, Tintin parachutes from the plane! But will he reach the meteorite before the other team?

BOOM!

Tintin wins the race to the meteorite! Despite dodging giant mushrooms (like the one from the original front cover, shown on the next page) and a monstrous spider, the brave reporter manages to rescue a piece of the meteorite before it sinks beneath the waves of the Arctic Ocean. Just as Tintin brings it on board the *Aurora*—BOOM! Another mushroom explodes!

A REAL CHUNK OF METEORITE

Do you remember the real-life story of the meteor that blew up over the region of Hainaut, Belgium, in 1934 (page 8)? Well, here is a piece of it! Analysis shows that it is an H chondrite—a stone meteorite with an iron content of around 27 percent. But it is not as big as the lump that Tintin saves for Professor Phostle—it only measures 1 inch across!

Not to scale

TINTIN'S GRAND ADVENTURE

In *The Shooting Star*, a lot of the story takes place on a ship. A maritime backdrop was a great way for Hergé to keep Captain Haddock (who first appeared in the previous adventure, *The Crab with the Golden Claws*) on board for Tintin's adventures. The next two adventures, *The Secret of the Unicorn* and *Red Rackham's Treasure*, are all about pirates, shipwrecks and ancient treasure—perfect stories for the captain to take part in!

Trivia: *The Shooting Star*

One more thing about Belgian scientists: it was a Belgian priest and physicist named Georges Lemaître (1894–1966) who first proposed the now widely-accepted theory of the origin of the universe: the Big Bang.

It is interesting that Hergé drew mushrooms growing on the meteorite. Mushroom spores are so small and tough that some people think they could have reached Earth from space, but it is unlikely that Hergé would have heard about this theory.

Hergé made a small mistake on page 21. In the second and third strips Captain Haddock has three stripes on his sleeve; in the fourth strip he has only two stripes!

Hergé's style of drawing—using simple lines and uniform colour—became known as "clear line" drawing. Throughout Tintin's adventures, Hergé almost never uses shading, but at the beginning of The Shooting Star, he draws a lot of shadows to imply the intensity of the light from the incoming meteor.

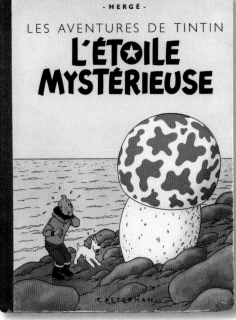

The original cover for *The Shooting Star* (1942)

GO ON MORE ADVENTURES WITH TINTIN!

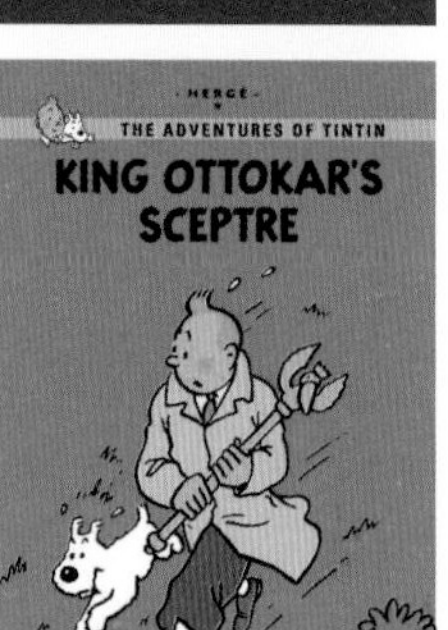

ALSO AVAILABLE

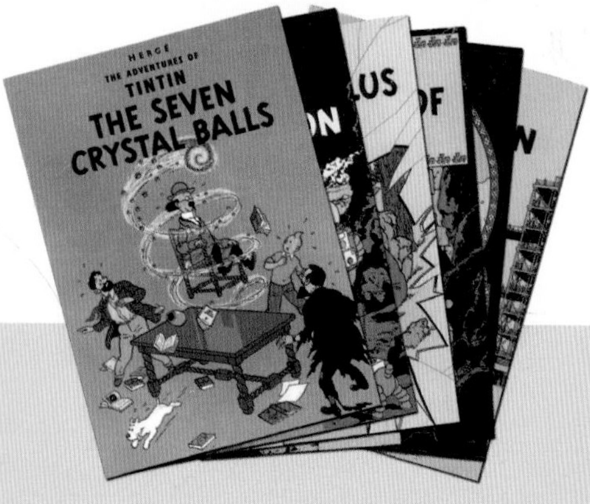

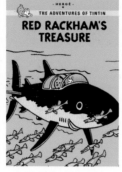

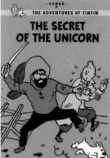